Stocks

For Retirees

Edition 2

Tony Pow

Why you want to read this book

It should improve your financial health substantially in the long run.

- A best seller was written by a young writer whose main income was from his books and none from his investing. His book is good for beginners or you want to brush up your English. My major income is from investing.

- Most books on this topic do not consider cash or money market fund as a sector. The average loss in the last two market plunges is about 45%. When the market is plunging, cash is the best investment.

- I select proven ideas from more than 100 books besides my original ideas and experiences. I also include links to current articles that will bring more depth to the topic. It is not a novel or documenting the story of my life. All related chapters are grouped in a section for easy future reference. Some chapters are not easy to digest as they have a lot of pointers and some may require you to try them out yourself.

- Check out my success stories.
  http://tonyp4idea.blogspot.com/2015/09/successes.html

- Many popular books claiming the authors making millions. However, usually their techniques are hard to follow. Many even admitted they had been bankrupted many times. Hence, their chance of bankrupting again is very high. Is bankruptcy fine with you? I cannot afford bankruptcy past and present. My techniques minimize the risk in investing.

- This book is about 220 pages (6*9) and I do not waste your time in narrating the story of my life. Many 100-page books could turn into just a few pages of useful information after the narrating the story of the author's life.

  If you buy the paperback version from Amazon.com, you may be eligible for a free Kindle version; check availability.

My motivation to write this book is sharing my experiences, both bad and good. I provide simple-to-follow techniques using the free (or low-cost) resources available to us. I have been successful in investing for decades. I am enjoying a comfortable financial life. I do not hold back my 'secrets' as my children are not interested in investing. It is my small legacy in sharing my investing ideas.

If you are looking how to make 100% return overnight, there are many other books claiming to do so and this book is not for you and many books written by authors who have never make money in the stock market. Ensure those books that are readable but only have a few pages specific on the topic. This book describes how to be a 'turtle' investor making fortune gradually and surely.

As everything in life, there is no guarantee this book will make you money. However, the chance of success will be substantially improved especially when you practice on most of the ideas presented in this book.

My articles in SeekingAlpha.com.
Click the link (http://seekingalpha.com/author/tony-pow/articles).

Why you invest

You need to learn about investing sooner or later in your life. You need to take some calculated risks.

Compare the returns of the following assets: cash, CDs, treasury bills, bonds, real estate and stocks. We start with the risk-free investments and end with the riskiest. It turns out that the average returns are in the opposite order. Cash and CDs are not risk-free as inflation eats our profits. For example, the real return is negative for the 2% return in a CD and a 3% inflation rate. In addition you have to pay taxes for the 'returns'. Our capitalist system punishes us for not taking risk.

There are two kinds of risk: blind risk and calculated risk. If you buy a stock due to a recommendation from a commentator on TV or a tip, most likely you are taking a blind risk. It would be the same in buying a house without thoroughly evaluating the house and its neighborhood. When you buy stocks with a proven strategy (i.e. when/what stocks to buy and when/what stocks to sell), you are taking a calculated risk. In the long run, stocks with calculated and educated risks are profitable.

Be a turtle investor by investing in value stocks and holding for longer time periods (a year or more). "Buy and Monitor" is better an approach than "Buy and Hold" as some could lose all the stock values such as in the failure of Enron.

For experienced investors, shorting, short-term trading and covered calls would make you good profits. Simple market timing would reduce your losses during market down turns. If you buy a market ETF and use my simple market timing, you should have beaten the market by a wide margin from 2000 to 2019.

With so many frauds and poor management, do not trust anyone with your investing. Do not buy investing instruments that are highly marketed such as annuity and term insurance.

If you are a handy man and do not mind to satisfy the constant requests of your tenants, buy real estate in growing areas could be very profitable in the long run. Take advantage of the tax laws such as investing in a 401K especially the part that is matched by your company and/or a Roth IRA.

Outline on how to start

1. First determine your risk tolerance, how much time you have for investing, your knowledge in investing and your portfolio size. When the market is risky, do not buy any stock.

2. Ensure the screened stocks are fundamentally sound.

3. Sell the stock when it fulfills your objective or the market is plunging.

4. Paper test your strategy.

5. When it is thoroughly tested out and the result is good, use real money slowly and gradually. Monitor your performance.

While most of my predictions are materialized, some are not. Learn from the arguments for the predictions, not the predictions themselves. When the predictions are based on educated guesses, more of them will be materialized in the long run. I do not use predictions after-the-fact as many do.

Filler: Wearing two hats

My bad experience is 911. I sold off many of my stocks via stops. The market came back in a few days and I did not buy them back. I was too emotional and forgot I was an investor too.

We may wear two hats: one as an emotional human being and one as a 'greedy' investor. If we feel guilty of taking advantage of the situation, just donate our 'loots' to charities.

Contents

My incredible returns

Here are my three proofs for my incredible returns. Many of the techniques are described in this book in general term. I am not a rich man as I am very conservative today.

Making 50% in one month

I claim to have the best one-month performance ever for recommending 8 or more stocks without using options and leverage. My following return is 57% in a month or 621% annualized. They are slightly different as I calculated the average from the averages of three different accounts. The average buy date is 12/26/18 and the "current date" after a month is 01/28/19 (Monday).

The performance may not be repeated. I will use the same screen for the coming years and even the expected 10% (or 120% annualized) is still very good.

I used the same screen for searching stock candidates and then evaluated the top searched stocks. I spent a total of about 20 hours from Dec. 15, 2018 to Jan. 5, 2019.

Stock	Buy Price	Sold or Current Price	Buy date	Sold or Current date	Profit %	Profit % Ann.	Status
CHK	2.13	2.99	01/03/09	01/18/19	40%	982%	Sold
MNK	16.41	21.45	01/03/19	01/25/19	31%	510%	Sold
MNK	16.43	21.45	01/03/19	01/25/19	31%	507%	Sold
NNBR	5.68	8.58	12/26/18	01/28/19	51%	565%	
NNBR	5.72	8.58	12/26/18	01/28/19	66%	727%	
ESTE	4.35	6.45	12/26/18	01/18/19	48%	766%	Sold
LCI	4.61	8.29	12/21/18	01/28/19	80%	767%	
MDR	8.01	9.13	01/08/19	01/28/19	14%	255%	
YRCW	3.29	5.78	12/21/18	01/28/19	76%	727%	
YRCW	3.26	5.78	12/21/18	01/28/19	77%	742%	
ASRT	3.56	4.18	12/26/18	01/28/19	17%	193%	
UTCC	7.13	11.00	12/26/18	01/28/19	54%	600%	
YRCW	2.92	5.78	12/26/18	01/28/19	98%	1083%	

Best one-year return

I claim to have the best-performed article in Seeking Alpha, an investing site, for recommending 15 or more stocks in one year after the publish date without using options and leverage. The link is:

https://seekingalpha.com/article/1095671-amazing-returns-velti-alcatel-lucent-alpha-natural-resources

The following link is how I calculated the return.

http://seekingalpha.com/article/2492255-a-tale-of-2-portfolios

My sector performance

As of 3/2019, my investment in my sector rotation account is about 5 times I invested. The fund has been held for many years. It proves nothing on performance but sector rotation works for me. It is complicated to calculate the annualized returns as the funds were added two times and I did not track those dates.

Recommended to dump FAANG and many more

On 8/5/2017 while FAANG had gained 50% in the last year, I recommended to dump them when the momentum changed. Three months later it lost 17% as a group while SPY (the market to many) gained 5%. Recommended to buy crude oil at $30 in Jan., 2016 and recommended to buy Apple in June, 2013.

https://tonyp4idea.blogspot.com/2018/10/faang-as-of-852017.html

#Fillers:

#Filler: Illogical logic

If we do not test for the pandemic, we would have zero increase in this pandemic. Some silly folks buy this argument. What happens to the once-great country?

#Filler: Ambition is good

That is what I heard from the web. The little girl wanted to be a president when she grew up. After attending a circus, she wanted to be a clown. Her smart father told her that she could be both.

Introduction

This book is targeted to retirees, conservative investors and/or couch potatoes who do not want to spend a lot of time in managing their investments.

This book helps someone looking for simple but profitable strategies in investing. It only takes about half an hour a month to monitor the market and decide what stocks to buy and sell.

We can reduce risk in investing by:

- Market Timing via simple technical indicators that are readily available free and simple to use.

  We do not want to invest when the market is plunging. As of 2014, we have two market plunges with an average loss of about 45% since 2000.

- Market Timing for stocks and sectors.

- Select best fundamental and technical stocks to buy.

- Select safer sectors.

- Diversify via stocks in different sectors and ETFs.

- Produce income via dividends and covered calls.

- A profitable and safe strategy.

- Avoid pitfalls and common mistakes. Also monitor our performances and identify mistakes.

- Write and stick with a customized trade plan to make investing a discipline and reduce emotion interference.

This book uses the advanced strategies described in my other books but in very simplified instructions. This book is similar with my other book "Conservative Investing". It has specific chapters for retirees and the two books will have different contents.

This book concentrates in investing. There is a specific chapter for handling financial topics for retirees. There are many books in the book at very low cost. Most likely their hidden agenda is to sell you other products /services for retirees such as estate plans, financial services and reversed mortgage. Some even offer free meals in expensive restaurants. This book tries not to duplicate these topics.

I am not a writer but a retail investor similar to most of you. I've been making a comfortable living via my investment ideas that I'm sharing in this book.

Some of the strategies described here have been used in my book Best Stocks 2014, According to Me. From 12/16/13 (the publish date) to 3/4/14, the list of all 135 selected stocks beat SPY (an ETF simulating the S&P 500) by 103% and the list of 9 small cap stocks beat SPY by 500% without considering dividends and compounding.

This book has 10 sections.

This book uses the advanced strategies described in my other books but in very simplified instructions. This book is almost identical to my other book Conservative Stock Investing. Future versions will be expanded specific to the book titles.
I start with investment advices. It will be easy read.

The next sections start with 'Do'. You have to try out how to work on market timing. They are the easiest ways to harvest the more advanced concepts. There may be one or two chapters after the 'Do' chapter to explain the 'Do'.

You should not buy any stocks when the market is plunging. Actually you should sell most of the stocks you own when the market is plunging. I have a simple way to spot market plunges. It is based on charts. However, you can obtain similar info without creating charts. Even with charts, there is nothing to subscribe or buy.

The chart also tells us when to reenter the market for the best opportunity to make money. I did well in 2003 and 2009.

Corrections provide opportunities to buy stocks. However, you have to prepare for the next correction by accumulating cash in advance and preparing a list of stocks you want to buy and at what prices. If you do not have such a list, just buy one or more ETFs.

In a nutshell, Tom's Strategy buys stocks in the Early Recovery (a stage defined by me) of the market cycle only and remains in cash after. It works since 2000. Be less conservative according to your risk tolerance by using covered calls, stop loss orders (during risky periods) and other provisions.

For starters, just trade ETFs and you can skip the latter chapters in evaluating stocks.

In the simplest terms, I discussed how to evaluate stocks fundamentally and technically. Use the research available in the free sites such as finviz.com and MSN Money. Instead of spending hours in researching one stock, you can do the same in a few minutes as others have researched them for you.

Many of my other books are mentioned for future references. You do not need to read them now unless you want to further your education in investing. Actually this book provides a lot of information including the entire bonus section for more advanced study.

If you want to buy stocks besides ETFs without a lot of research, try out the following book or the more recent book in this series: Best Stocks 2014, According to Me (not a promise for a later book).

The other book is "Complete the art of investing", which this book is based on; the Kindle version has over 850 pages (6*9). It covers most topics in investing.

I am not a writer but a retail investor similar to most of you. I've been making a comfortable living via my investment ideas that I'm sharing in this book.

Some of the strategies described here have been used in my book Best Stocks 2014, According to Me. From 12/16/13 (the publish date) to 3/4/14, the list of all 135 selected stocks beat SPY (an ETF simulating the S&P 500) by 103% and the list of 9 small cap stocks beat SPY by 500% without considering dividends and compounding.

Retail investors have a lot of advantages over fund managers. However, I advise not to be a trader especially day traders for beginners. Statistically most amateur traders lose money as they cannot compete with experienced, disciplined traders. Even if you study several good books by great traders, you will still lose money initially. No books can replace the actual trading experience.

My books do not teach you to be a trader but a 'turtle' investor.

How this book is organized

Most graphs and tables are in landscape orientation for both paperback and e-readers. Some graphs may not be displayed adequately on a small screen of an e-reader. E-readers may be available in the current version of Windows, so you can read e-books on the larger screen of your PC. For better orientation, just flip the e-readers 90 degrees.

A link is usually included for these screens. Copy it to your browser to display the graphs on your PC if desirable. Instructions on how to produce some graphs are provided as you should try them out. One example is how to produce a chart on detecting market crashes.

It is easier to display some tables in landscape mode. Select a table or a graph via your e-reader to display it to fit the screen.

The font size and page size of most e-book formats can be adjusted. The unknown, special character is the "smiling face" that the current Kindle does not convert correctly as of this writing.

There are clickable links to web articles. Most of them are from my own web sites and public web sites such as Wikipedia. Some public links may not be available in the future as they are not under my control and my book offerings may change.

Fidelity Video provides video clips to explain some basic terms and it may require Fidelity customers to sign on in order to view them. Check the trial offer from Fidelity. YouTube offers similar video lessons.

These links extend the usefulness of this book by making available specific topics that may not be interesting to every reader. It also provides articles (most are not written by me) for more in-depth analyzes.

The current version provides most of the links the paperback readers can enter into your browser. Get the same information by entering a search in Wikipedia such as Dogs of Dow.

Investopedia is another source beside Wikipedia.
http://www.investopedia.com/

'Afterthoughts' includes my additional comments and comments from others. Readers can make comments in this book's website. These comments may be included in the Afterthoughts in subsequent revisions, with the commenter's last name redacted. It is the section of the article for freer and informal discussion. It also contains some political and social issues.

There are fillers with tips and jokes (most original) to fill up the empty space of the printed book. Fillers, links and afterthoughts may disrupt the flow of reading this book. However, no readers so far ask me to take them out.

For convenience, this book uses SPY, an Exchange Traded Fund (ETF) simulating the S&P 500, as the benchmark for the market.

Annualized returns (Return * 365 / (Days between)) are used where appropriate for more meaningful comparison. To illustrate, I have a 10% return in 6 months, a 10% in a year and a 10% in 2 years. It is more meaningful to use annualized returns of 20%, 10% and 5% respectively for the 6-month return, the one-year return and the 2-year return in this example.

Usually I do not include the dividend, so you can add an estimated 1.5% to the annualized return. In addition, compound interest is not used for easier calculation, so the actual return could be even better.

This book is a new version of the book Stock Investing for Retirees.

Fast track
Read the following chapters first: Chapter 10, 16 and 18. Then select interesting topics. Skip the advanced topics for now.

For beginner investors

Follow the same advice for couch potatoes as above. Read basic investment articles for beginners. Both Fidelity and AAII (both require being a client or a member) have excellent articles. Alternatively, buy a book for beginners. To include all the basic terms and concepts, I have to double the size of this book which is already lengthy and bore most readers who already have the basic knowledge.

Click here for Morningstar classroom.
http://morningstar.com/cover/classroom.html

Click here for Fidelity basic in investing.
https://www.fidelity.com/investment-guidance/investing-basics

About the author

I graduated from Cal. State University at San Jose in Industrial Engineering and University of Mass. in Amherst with a MS in Industrial Engineering. I have retired from a job in IT. I have been an investor for over 30 years.

Dedication

To all retail investors and future retail investors including my grandchildren.

Acknowledgement

Poi for gathering my research info and working on the business side of the book.

Important notices

Version 1. 12/2014. 2.3 12/2021.

Printed version. ISBN-13:978-1505245486 ISBN-10:1505245486

Disclaimer

Do not gamble with money that you cannot afford to lose. Past performance is a guideline and is not necessarily indicative of future results. All information is believed to be accurate, but there is not a guarantee. All the strategies including charts to detect market plunges described have no guarantee that they will make money and they may lose money. Do not trade without doing due diligence and be warned that most data may be obsolete. All my articles and the associated data are for informational and illustration purposes only. I'm not a professional investment counselor, a tax professional or any other field. Seek one before you make any investment decisions. Remember to consult with a registered financial adviser before making any investment decisions. The above mentioned also applies for all other advice such as on accounting, taxes, health and any topic mentioned in this book. Tax laws change all the time, so talk to your tax advisors before taking any action. Most of the time, I use annualized for a better comparison; 5% in a month is more than 4% in a year for example. For simplicity, most of my returns do not include commissions, exchange fees, order spread and dividends. It is the same for all the links contained in this book. Some articles may offend some one or some organization unintentionally. If I did, I'm sorry about that. I am politically and religiously neutral. I have provided my best efforts to ensure the accuracy of my articles. Data also from different sources was believed to be accurate. However, there is no guarantee that they are accurate and suitable for the current market conditions and /or your individual situations. The values of some parameters such as RSI(14) are arbitrarily set by me. My publisher and I are not liable for any damages in using this book or its contents.

Section I: Simple techniques

For starters, just trade ETFs such as SPY (an ETF simulating the market), and you can skip the rest of the book. It only take a few minutes every month. When the market is not plunging, buy or keep SPY (or any ETF that stimulates the market); otherwise sell it. Do the opposite when the market is recovering.

If you have less than $50,000 to invest, just buy ETFs. Improve your investing skills by reading investment articles from this book and your broker's web site. For example, Fidelity has a lot of information for investors.

Subscription to AAII is recommended. When your portfolio grows more than $50,000, invest on a subscription such as Value Line, GuruFocus, Zacks or IBD (more for momentum traders). Initially, use the information for paper trading on value stocks, which is usually available from brokers.

For the long term, knowledge is most important in your investing life and experience comes next. Retail investors have a lot of advantages over fund managers. However, I advise you NOT to be a trader. Hence, you should ignore the 'fabulous' trade systems that claim to be very profitable. Statistically most amateur traders lose money as they cannot compete with experienced, disciplined traders.

How to start

I recommend trading ETFs first and when the market is not risky. The very basic terms such as ETF are not fully explained here; try Investopedia for terms you need to know. Otherwise this book would be doubled in size and it would bore most readers. Investopedia, your broker's web site (especially Fidelity) and AAII (requiring subscription) provide many excellent articles. Alternatively, buy a book for beginners. Here are some freebies:

Click here for Morningstar classroom.
http://morningstar.com/cover/classroom.html
Click here for Vanguard.
https://investor.vanguard.com/investing/investor-education
Click here for Investopedia's Tutorials.
http://www.investopedia.com/university/
Click here for Yahoo!
http://finance.yahoo.com/education/begin_investing
Click here for Fidelity basic in investing.
https://www.fidelity.com/investment-guidance/investing-basics

1 Simplest market timing

Why market timing

Before 2000, market timing was a waste of time. However after that, we have had two market plunges with the average loss of about 45%. It sounds harder to time the market than it actually is. We have a simple technique to detect market plunges and when to reenter the market. Our objective is reducing the loss to 25%.

Market timing depends on charts; the following describes how to use chart information without creating charts. Most charts will not identify the peaks and bottoms of the market as they depend on data (i.e. the stock prices). However, it would reduce further loses. It is simpler than it sounds. Just follow the procedure below.

The first part of this technique detects market plunges, and the second part advises you when to reenter the market. It applies to individual stocks too.

How to detect market plunges without charts (a.k.a. Death Cross)

1. Bring up Finviz.com.

2. Enter SPY (or any ETF that simulates the market).

3. If SMA-200% is positive, it indicates that the market plunge has not been detected and you can skip the following steps.

4. The market is plunging if SMA-50% is more negative than SMA-200%. To illustrate this condition, SMA-200% is -2% and SMA-50% is -5%.

5. Sell most stocks starting with the riskiest ones first such as the ones with negative earnings, high P/Es and/or high Debt/Equity. Obtain this info from Finviz.com by entering the symbol of the stock you own.

6. Conservative investors should sell only those over-priced stocks. Aggressive investors should sell all stocks. Extremely aggressive

investors should sell all stocks, buy contra ETFs, and even short stocks. I do not recommend beginners to be aggressive.

When to return to the market (a.k.a. Golden Cross)

Use the above in a reversed sense to detect whether the market has been recovering. However, when the SMA-200% turns positive, I would start buying value stocks (low P/E but the 'E' has to be positive, and/or low Debt/Equity).

1. Bring up Finviz.com.

2. Enter SPY (or any ETF that simulates the market).

3. If SMA-200% is negative, the market is not recovering, and you can skip the following steps.

4. Sell all contra ETFs and close all shorts if you have any.

5. Market recovery is confirmed when SMA-50% is more positive than SMA-200%. To illustrate this condition, SMA-200% is 2% and SMA-50% is 5%. Commit a large percent of cash (or all cash for aggressive investors) to stocks. If you do not know what to buy, buy SPY or an ETF that simulates the market.

Do the above once a month. When the SPY price is closer to SMA actions percentage, perform the above once a week. The charts and data for market timing described in this book are based on SMA-350 (Simple Moving Average) that is more preferable than this simple procedure, but it requires some simple charting.

2 Quick analysis of ETFs

Evaluate an ETF

ETFs are a basket of stocks according to the market, a specific sector, country or a specific theme.

Yahoo!Finance used to give the P/E of an ETF. Try to get it from ETFdb.com. Enter the symbol of the ETF such as XLU, and then select Valuation. If it is below 15 and above zero, it could be a value ETF. Also, if the current price is lower than its NAV, it is sold at a discount (or premium vice versa). Compare its YTD Return to SPY's.

Alternatively, get similar info from http://www.multpl.com/. In addition, this web site provides the following metrics: Shiller P/E, Price/Sales, and Price/Book.

From Finviz.com, enter the ETF symbol. If SMA-20%, SMA-50% and SMA-200% are all positive, most likely the ETF is in an uptrend. To illustrate, SMA-200 is Simple Moving Average for the last 200 trading sessions (no trading on weekends and specific holidays). The percent is how much the stock price of the ETF is above the SMA. If the percent is negative, it means the stock price is below the SMA.

If your average holding period of your stocks is about 50 days, SMA-50% is more appropriate to you.

If RSI(14) > 65, it is probably over-sold; if it is < 30, it is probably under-sold (indicating value).

In addition, ensure the ETF's average volume is high (I suggest more than 10,000 shares), the market cap is more than 300 M, and it has low fees. Most popular ETFs have these characteristics. Beginners should avoid leveraged ETFs.

How to determine if the sector has been recovered

It is easier to profit by following the uptrend of an ETF using the above info. It is hard to detect when the bottom of an ETF has been reached. If SMA-20%, SMA-50% and SMA-200% are all positive, most likely the ETF is in an uptrend or it has recovered. It does not always happen as predicted, so use stops to protect your investment.

An example

First, determine whether the market is risky. Most beginners should not invest in a risky market. Advanced investors can bet against the market or a specific sector by buying contra ETFs or puts.

Next, you want to limit the number of sector ETFs by selecting those that are either in an uptrend or hitting bottom (bottom is hard to predict). Personally I prefer sectors with long-term uptrends (indicated by articles found in many web sites including cnnfn.com and Seeking Alpha.

For illustration purposes only for deteriorating market conditions, I would select the following ETFs: SPY (simulating the market based on large companies) and XLP (consumer staples). XLP should perform better than XLY (consumer discretionary) during a recession as those products are the necessities.

Technical indicators such as SMA-50 (Simple Moving Average for the last 50 sessions), SMA-200 and RSI(14) are obtained from Finviz.com and the rest are obtained from Yahoo!Finance.com. After you buy the ETF, use a stop loss to protect your investment. For example, bio tech sector moved up for many months until it crashed in 2015. Change the stop loss value every month to protect your gains in this case.

As of 2/5/2016	**SPY**	**XLP (Staples)**	**XLY (Discret.)**
Price	190	50	71
NAV	192	50	73
• **Technical**			
SMA-50	-4%	0%	-7%
SMA-200	-6%	2%	-7%
RSI(14)	44	50	36
Other	Double bottom at $186		
• **Fundamental**			
P/E	17	20	19
Yield	2.1%	2.5%	1.5%
YTD return	-5%	0.5%	-5%
Net asset	174 B	9 B	10 B

Explanation

- The figures may not be identical among web sites due to the dates they are using.
- XLY has best discount among the 3 ETFs as most investors believe a recession is coming.
- XLP has less down trend among the 3 ETFs as expected.
- XLY is more undersold among the three as expected.
- Double bottom is a technical pattern that indicates the stock would surge upward.
- SPY has a better value according to its P/E.
- XLY's dividend is the least among the three as they have more tech companies in the ETF. They have to plow back the profits to research and development.
- XLP has the best YTD return among the three.
- As long as the asset is above 500 M (200 M for specialized ETFs), it is fine and all three pass this mark.

There are many metrics such as Debt/Equity not readily available from most web sites. Many sites list the top holdings of a specific ETF. Just average the metrics of the top ten or so of its stock holdings.

An example

This example evaluates RING, a gold miner, using ETFdb and Finviz that are free from the web. The data is from July, 6, 2020.

Bring up ETFdb and enter RING in the search. There are basic info that are important to me: Sector (gold miners), Asset Size (Large-Cap), Issuer (iShares), Inception (Jan. 31, 2012), Expense Ratio (0.39%) and Tax Form (1099).

They fit all my requirements. The expense ratio is higher than most ETFs that simulating an index such as SPY. I try to trade ETFs using Tax Form 1099 in my taxable accounts. The large cap created about 8 years ago by a reputable company are good.

Select "Dividend and Valuation". P/E of 17.39 is fine in a rank of 11 in 27 in similar group of ETFs. As in my books, I stated it is hard to evaluate miners. I buy this ETF primarily to fight the possibility of inflation and the potential depreciation of USD. The dividend rate of 0.52% (0.70% from Finviz) is in the low range of the scale; it is fine for me as dividend is not my concern.

There are more info from this web site. For simplicity, bring up Finviz:

- The short-term trend is up (SMA-20% = 8% and SMA-50% = 7%).
- The long-term trend is up (SMA-200% = 26%).
- It is close to overbought (RSI(14) = 64%; 65% to me is overbought).
- It is -4% from 52-w High. It has performed well from the YTD, Last Year, Last Quarter, Last Month and Last Week.
- It almost doubles in price from mid March this year.
- Avg. Vol. is fine.

From ETFdb, check the Holding. It has 39 stocks, so it is quite diversified for this industry. The two top holdings are NEM (19%) and ABX (18%), which is listed as GOLD in NYSX. I also consider to buy these two stocks in addition to RING. You can estimate the other metrics that are not available by averaging these two stocks. Here is my summary:

STOCK	NEM	GOLD
Forward P/E	20	25
Debt / Share	0.31	0.24
ROE	17%	22%
Sales Q/Q	43%	30%
EPS Q/Q	389%	254%
SMA50	2%	4%
RSI(14)	59%	60%
Insider Trans	-13%	N/A
Fidelity's Equity Summary Score	6.1	6.8

3 Rotate four ETFs

We can beat the market by rotating one ETF that represents the market such as SPY and cash via market timing.

During a market uptrend, rotating the following four ETFs could be more profitable than staying with SPY (or any ETF that simulating the market). Be warned that a short-term capital gain in taxable accounts is not treated as favorably as the long-term capital gain; check current tax laws.

The allocation percentages depend on your individual risk tolerance. You can use indexed mutual funds. Compare their expenses and restrictions. Some mutual funds charge you if you withdraw within a specific time period.

Select the best performer of last month (from Seeking Alpha, cnnFn, or one of many ETF/mutual fund sites). Add a contra ETF such as SH to take advantage of a falling market for more aggressive investors. Add sector ETFs to the described four ETFs such as XLY, XLP, XLE, XLF, XLU, IYW, XHB, IYM, OIL and XLU to expand your selection.

ETFs	Money Market	U.S.	International	Bond
Fidelity		Spartan Total Market	Spartan Global Market	Spartan US Bond
Vanguard		Total Stock Market	Total International Market	Total Bond Market
My choice	Fidelity	SPY	Vanguard	Fidelity
Suggest %				
During Market plunge	90%	0%	0%	10%
After plunge	10%	60%	20%	10%

Explanation

- The above are suggestions only. If your broker offers similar ETFs, consider using them.

- Check out any restrictions of the ETFs and commissions.
- 4 ETFs (one actually is a money market fund) are enough for most starters. They are diversified, low-cost and you do not need rebalancing except during a market plunge.
- The percentages are suggestions only. If you are less risk tolerant, allocate more to a money market fund, CD and/or bond ETF.
- Have at least 10% allocated to the money market fund for safety.
- When the market is risky, reduce stock equities (i.e. increase money market and bond allocations).
- The symbols for Fidelity ETFs are FSTMX, FSGDX and FBIDX.
- The symbols for Vanguard ETFs are VTSMX, VGTSX and VBMFX.
- If you are more advanced, use additional sector ETFs to rotate. Also buy long-term bond funds (such as 30-year Treasury) when the interest rates is 10% or more.

4 Simplest way to evaluate stocks

Beginners should trade ETFs only. This chapter is for the readers who are ready or getting ready to trade stocks.

Many stock researches have already been done recently and some are available free of charge. I have no affiliation with Fidelity except I retired from it. You can open an account with them with no balance. Their Equity Summary Score is one of the best indicators; I check out **value** stocks with score higher than 8.

Several sources

The popular ones are Morningstar, Value Line, The Street and Zacks (currently free for rankings of individual stocks). If they are not free, check out whether they are available from your local library. I have 3 simple ways to evaluate stocks starting with the simplest. In addition, read the articles on the selected stocks from Fidelity, Finviz, Seeking Alpha and many other sources for further evaluation.

Fidelity

Select only stocks that have Fidelity's Equity Summary Score 8 or higher. There are tons of information about a stock.

A modified stock selection based on a magazine article

Most metrics are available from Finviz.

1. Forward P/E (expected earnings and not based on the last twelve months). It should range from 5 to 15 (10 to 25 for high tech stocks). EV/EBITDA (from Yahoo!Finance) is a better choice as it includes the debts and cash than P/E; it would be more effective if it uses forward earnings. If you do not use EV/EBITDA, ensure Debt/Equity is less than 0.5 except for the debt-intensive industries.

2. ROE (Return of Equity) measures how well the company uses the capital. I prefer stocks with ROE greater than 5%.

3. Volatility. Conservative investors should select stocks with a beta of less than one (i.e. less volatile).

4. Insider Transactions from should be less than 5%.

5. Momentum. Check out the SMA-50 (actually SMA-50%) and SMA-200. Ideally they should be positive. It is especially important for stocks you do not want to keep for a long time.

A simple scoring system using Finviz

Bring up Finviz.com and then enter the stock symbol.

No.	Metric	Good	Bad	Score
1	Forward P/E[1]	Between 2.5 and 12.5, Score = 2	> 50 or < 0, Score = -1	
2	P/ FCF[1]	< 12, Score = 1	>30 or < 0, Score = -1	
3	P/S[1]	< 0.8, Score = 1	< 0, Score = -1	
4	P/ B[1]	< 1, Score = 1	< 0, Score = -1	
	Compare quarter to quarter of last year			
5	Sales Q/Q	> 15%, Score = 1	< 0, Score = -1	
6	EPS Q/Q	> 20% , Score = 1	< 0, Score = -1	
			Grand Score	
	Stock Symbol Date[2]	Current Price	SPY	

Footnote

1 Negative values for Sales (due to accounting adjustments), Equity and Book are possible but not likely.

2 The last row is for your information only. SPY is used to measure whether it will beat the market by comparing the return of this stock to the return of SPY.

The Score

Score each metric and sum up all the scores giving the Grand Score. If the Grand Score is 3, the stock passes this scoring system. Even if it is a 2, it still deserves further analysis if you have time. You may want to add scores from other vendors. To illustrate on using Fidelity, add 1 to the score if Fidelity's Equity Summary score is 8 or higher. Monitor the performance after every 6 months or so to see whether this scoring system beats the market.

Very basic advice for beginners

Beginners should stick with U.S. stocks with Market Cap greater than 800 M (million), Debt/Equity less than .25 (25%) except for debt-intensive industries such as utilities and airlines and Forward P/E between 5 to 20 (25 for high-tech companies). These metrics are all available from Finviz.com, which is free.

Do not have more than 20% of your portfolio in one stock (unless it is an ETF or mutual fund) and do not have more than 30% of your portfolio in one sector.

For more conservative investors, buy non-volatile stocks whose beta (available from Yahoo!Finance) is less than 1. Beta of 1 represents the market (the S&P 500 index). For example, a stock with beta 1.5 statistically fluctuates more than 50% of the market and hence it is very volatile.

Try paper trading to check out your strategy and your skill in trading stocks. If your broker does not provide one, use a spreadsheet to record your trades or check the availability of simulator.investopedia.com.

Filler 12 noon is not 12 pm

The Chinese restaurant I went to says they are open at 12 am. Are they wrong or is the world wrong?

The next hour after 11 am is 12 am, NOT 12 pm. The one who set it up did it totally wrong and no one complains about it until now. If I were born earlier, I would have corrected it.

Section II: Investment advices

We need to distinguish useful information from garbage.

1 The advantages of a retail investor

Why we, the retail investors, can beat the professional fund managers? It is not likely if you consider all those research resources they have. It is likely after you read this article. However, in reality, the average retail investor does not beat the market due to switching between stocks and cash at the wrong time. Via the greed, they invest in the peak of the market and via fears they divest in the bottom. They do not expect the market would return in the bottom but it always does.

Most fund managers are smarter than I, better educated in investing than I, have ten times more research tools than I and have ten times more computer power than I. However, most of them do not beat me, the average casual retail investor. In addition, I spend less time in stock research than an average fund manager (working at least 60 hours a week) - I have a life too and they don't. ☺

It could be:

- They cannot beat the market all the time. When they do, money flows in and vice versa. It is very hard for them to perform with extraordinary cash. When everyone is cashing in their funds, they need to sell stocks even though they have stocks with good fundamentals and/or better potential to appreciate.

  The saying "When there is blood in the streets, most likely it is the best time to buy" is correct. 2009 is a recent example. Fund managers cannot take advantage of this opportunity.

- Most cannot play market timing freely and they have to satisfy all the rules set up for the fund. Every time they want to buy a stock, they need to ensure no rules set up for the fund have been broken such as a restricted percent of a stock to the fund. Most funds prohibit their managers to short, buy contra ETFs and/or maintain high cash position. Basically, most are not allowed to react to a market going up or down.

- When they trade, their high volumes are tracked by day traders who can ride on their wagon. Hence they have to pay more to buy and get less to sell.

- By my rough estimate, they have about 1,000 stocks (about 600 for larger funds) to deal with. I as a retail investor have about 3,000 stocks even skipping most stocks with prices below $2 or not listed in the three major exchanges.

  Their stocks have been fully evaluated by analysts and newsletters / subscriptions such as Value Line and /or some firms specializing in stock research for them. Hence, they do not gain any advantage by following their peers.

  The small and mid-cap stocks are risky but are more rewarding statistically. Many fund managers cannot buy them due to the sizes of their funds.

- Their performance as a group is actually worse. Some bad mutual funds close and their bad performances are not added to the average performance of all mutual funds. It is termed as survivorship bias. Those funds closed due to frauds could lose all money invested.

- Not nimble enough.
  By the time, when they have done all the research and received the approval to buy a specific stock, I may have bought the stock already. Usually it takes at least a week for a large fund to complete trading a stock.

- The high expenses.
  The fee is about 1.5% for an average fund. The expenses are 2% plus 20% on the profit for an average hedge fund (Chapter 8). When the fund also owns the broker, watch out how it can make its brokerage arm more profitable by jacking up the fees. The hedge fund's usual 20% on the profit encourages its fund managers to take bigger risks.

- Not spend enough time to do own research.
  Most do not spend enough time on basic research and figure why some strategies work and some do not at certain market conditions. They spend a lot of time in following the fund's and the company's objectives, rules and regulations. One fund

manager with over 30 year career did not do more research than I in 5 years.

- Wrong objective.
  The objective of most funds is beating the common index after expenses. Most fund managers do not want to take too much risk and their personal objective is job security. One will not lose the job if his performance is similar to a target index.

  My objective is to beat the index by a good margin at acceptable risk.

- Most likely their good performance could be due to taking too much unnecessary risk and high leverage. Their performances improve when the market is good, but degrade when the market is down. When I see the market is coming down, I would park more cash and I only use leverage when the market is going up.

- It is like a thousand monkeys banging on the keyboard to find stocks. At least one can find a winning stock. This is what happens to a new crop of analysts. They believe they can eventually find a winner in stock pickers by elimination. They ignore that luck has a lot to do with their performance. When winners are selected by pure luck, the selection process is wrong and the future results will not be consistent.

- They buy the same stocks as their peers are buying. If they do not perform within a certain range of a benchmark, they get canned. Hence, they stay away from risky stocks that usually have better profits. We pay them to research these risky stocks to separate the gems from garbage, not to follow the herd of their peers.

- Retail investors have a lot of advantages over fund managers. However, I advise not to be traders especially day traders for beginners. Statistically most amateur traders lose money as they cannot compete with experienced, disciplined traders. My books do not teach you to be a trader.

2 Retirees, take notice

When we retire or are being laid off, we have plenty of time. It is bad not to do anything. However, the worst could happen to us: We invested in some venture without due diligence and lost our entire savings. There are so many real-life examples.

Every one eats out and enjoys it. Some believe they can do a better job by opening a new restaurant. It is human nature to be overly optimistic even on this toughest business and those who surround him or her, do not want to dampen that enthusiasm. Most new ventures fail miserably. Eating out and running a restaurant are completely different.

Investing in stocks is another popular one. Many take a course in day trading. If their system works that well, why do they want to show it to you? When you want to invest in stocks, you should have many years of investing experience and do not gamble with the money you cannot afford to lose. Unless you're a Congress person using insiders' info (not any more now), the market is unpredictable.

One retiree lost all his money in the stock market which has too much volatility, and died because of worries. After several years, the market revived but he did not.

One retired headmaster worked as a partner in a small brokerage firm. Despite having fame and fortune initially, never-the-less he eventually lost all his money. He executed an order without checking his client's maximum bet allowed. The bet was a total loss and this verbal order based on trust could not be legally bound.

The retired and famous baseball player from Boston lost all his money from owning a company that made video games. Even though he was an excellent baseball player, he was not a business man and his failure was almost a sure thing. For every successful story, there must be more failures that are not publicized. In most cases, no ambition is the best ambition during our retirement. Investing in something we do not understand will likely cost us money, effort, frustration, and even our health.
Withdrawing 401Ks and IRAs.
(http://tonyp4idea.blogspot.com/2012/09/withdrawing-iras.html)

3 Advice for a 70 year old

Why do you being a 70-year old want to be richer? By statistics, which never lie, you have about ten years to live plus or minus five days☺. Investing is very emotional and it can damage your health. Inheritance is good for the next generation, but it should not be your primary reason to make more money. In addition, it would take out their objective in life and fun in creating wealth. They should inherit enough to start something and nothing more.

I agree that we ought to constantly keep our minds active. However, you're competing with veteran professionals in the stock market. Do not turn your life savings into a very expensive hobby. One way to beat them is to invest when everyone is selling and vice versa. It is easier said than done.

If you could live to your eighth decade, you've beaten the odds and the social security system which was designed that a population will not live that long. Just have a big smile and a fulfilling day. Do not let the market control your mood. Like my late mother said: Every day you wake up alive and feel no pain, you've earned another day that is more important than all the gold in the world☺.

Afterthoughts

- Bala said:

Great words from your late mom. Even at 70, learning never stops and I learned something today. Thanks.

- Norman:

Many of us in the 70 year old category are forced to support our children and their children during this depression. My reason for making money is to keep them eating and allow the children to go to school and college.

- Advice to a friend starting a new business. http://tonyp4idea.blogspot.com/2014/05/starting-music-business.html

4 Is Social Security going to survive?

Contrary to popular belief, Social Security will not run out of cash. However, it will be cut down in purchase power. It is supposed to adjust to inflation. The inflation rate has been manipulated by the government by using the CPI that does not account for food and energy.

Our politicians will not allow Social Security to bankrupt otherwise they'll not be re-elected. Some simple steps with some comic relief are:

- Move money to Social Security from budgets in other areas and currently we do only have a debt ceiling and no need to balance the budget.
- Printing more money and/or beg China or anyone to loan us more. China should be smarter by now not to fall into the same trap.
- From China's latest espionage, the U.S. citizens would not object to sell their country to China for a million dollar to each citizen. China figures out the 1 million could turn into buying power of $1,000 next year and they can tax 99% of the windfall payment.
- Tax more on citizens like the extra tax for Social Security, Medicare, any taxes... and add a new tax called VAT.
- Tax the rich until they move out of this country. Then we will have a new tax named exit tax. It is similar to killing the goose that lays the golden eggs.
- Import more young and hard-working foreigners. Ensure not to import their parents to collect welfare Social Security Supplement which could defeat the original purpose.
- Selective immigration would allow more income and investment.
- Reduce the aged population with fast food deals for seniors, early bird specials, more legalized, addictive drugs specific for

seniors, unlimited alcohol for seniors (killing seniors in the car and other seniors on the street), guns for recreation for seniors, free sex for folks over 70 every night at all senior centers... ☺

As long as they die happy, everyone is happy.

- Incentive to die early.
  If they suffer, let them die peacefully. How about one extra percent exemption for each year below life expectancy? They may not know there is no requirement to file income tax on the year they die. The last two years usually requires the most expensive health care, not to mention the physical suffering. ☺

- Give seniors Viagra free.
  It will make prostitutes fully employed with new customers from this age group. Excessive sexual exercise will end their lives earlier but happily. Not a personal experience but an observation. LOL.

Afterthoughts

Most points are valid but some are just for your enjoyment. I wrote this on a rainy day and needed something to cheer me up. Sorry if this blog offends anyone.

Articles on Quirks. http://www.marketwatch.com/story/how-to-profit-from-social-securitys-quirks-2014-08-07

Filler: Tips

Penny stocks are risky as many do not have information required by SEC and the major exchanges. They are traded over the counter, OTC. They cannot be shorted (and most likely you do not want to do so even it was allowed). Pier 1, Ford, American Airlines and many others were all penny stocks.

Expect one winner for several losers. However, the total profit could outpace the total loss if the strategy is properly implemented.

5 Newsletters and subscriptions

I've been using investment newsletters / subscriptions for years. Many are priced reasonably and some are even free. While a lot of them are garbage, some are very good.

When you have a lot of money to invest and you're not using a financial adviser and/or not subscribing to any investment service, it could be a big financial mistake. You do not want to be penny smart but pound foolish. However, you could be among the few exceptions if you have the knowledge and time to make use of the free financial data, guidance and articles from the web.

You need a computer, access to Internet and a spreadsheet in order to use most subscription services effectively.

I'm not going to compare specific systems / newsletters, but will include general pointers on how to select them. Yesterday's garbage could be a gold mine today if the subscription improves and/or the market conditions fit what they recommend.

First, you need to find what you need and how much time you can afford to use them. If you have $20,000 or less to invest, most likely you just buy an ETF such as SPY as your investment both in money and time will not pay off.

Here are some pointers.

- Newsletters giving you specific stocks to buy do not require much of your time. However, if they're successful, there will be too many followers buying the same stocks to drive up the prices of the recommended stocks at least temporarily. The owner and his insiders will buy the recommended stocks before you. I had several of this kind of newsletter, and so far I have not renewed any one of them.

- If I found the Holy Grail in investing, do you believe I'll share it with you for $100 or so? I only will after I invest my findings first. My subscribers would push up the prices for me and then I unload them before them.

- If the volumes of the recommended stocks are small, they can be manipulated easily either by the newsletter owners and/or by your peer subscribers. The first ones to sell the recommended stocks win and the last ones to sell lose.

- I prefer systems that can find a lot of stocks by providing many searches (same as screens). However, it will take a lot of time to learn and test their performances that would require a historical database. Most likely, you need to further research on each stock screened. The service would select a limited number of stocks for further analysis, so it will save time.

  From my experience, the best performance comes from the stocks that have been screened by more than one search especially for shorter term (less than 6 months). My theory is that they've been identified by more folks and the buyers jack up the prices. There will be more profits to buy them ahead of the herd and sell them before the herd.

- We all receive promotional mails that they could at least triple the return of your investment. Just ignore them. If it is that good, most likely they will keep them for themselves. Same for seminars to boost some penny stocks. Sometimes the recommended stocks will rise initially to lure you and other suckers to move it. Watch out!

- A 'guru' told me that he made a big fortune in silver a month ago. Guess what? He also recommended selling it two months ago and lost a lot of money in doing so. He is always right but he will not advertise the times he was wrong. We call it a double talk technique.

- There are free (or deeply discounted) subscription services. Take advantage of them. Some services require you to spend a lot of time, so ensure you have the time. Keep track of the performance yourself via paper trading.

- Subscribe the newsletter to fit your style of investing. If you're a day trader, newsletters on long-term investment are not good for you. Some subscriptions handle all kinds of investing styles and you need to find the strategies and recommendations to fit your style.

- Newsletters on penny stocks are most likely too risky for most of us. I define penny stocks as less than $2 and a market cap less than 100 M. However, I do buy stocks with prices around $2 in stock price or a capital cap less than 100 M. Actually I bought ALU at $1 but ALU's market cap then was about 2 billion. The stocks with prices between $1 and $10 represent the most volatile and some are real, ignored gems as most analysts do not do research on them.

- There are many sectors like drugs, mines and banks that we cannot evaluate effectively ourselves. It is better to seek expert advices.

- Remember there is no free lunch in life. The higher potential return of a stock is, the riskier the stock is.

- Some newsletters / subscriptions save us time by summarizing the financial data like a value rank and a growth rank. When the market favors growth, you use the growth rank (vs. a value rank), and vice versa.

- Be careful on the commercials particularly from radio in selling to peoples' fears and their greed by overstating without necessarily telling the whole story. There is no free lunch. It is not possible to make 25% in covered calls consistently or making another gold rush from $400 to $1,800.

- TV financial shows usually exaggerate in order to sell their staffs. Analyze before you act on the news.

- As a retail investor, most of us cannot afford to do extensive researches. Many researches and market opinions are available in the internet free. Start to search such information from your broker's site.

- Do not trust the performances of the newsletter providers. There are many ways to manipulate their performances.

- Most compare their performances with S&P 500. It is legal for investment newsletters to inflate their performance with dividends while comparing to an index without dividends.

To illustrate, for the last 10 years, S&P 500 has an average annual return of 1% on appreciation and 1.5% on dividends for a total return of 2.5%. Hence, the performance should compare to 2.5% not 1%.

- The performance of last 10 years is more important than that of 25 years. Their method of stock evaluation / ranking hopefully has been improved. In addition, the last 10 years is a better prediction of the newsletter than the last 25 years.

- When the new major researcher takes over the subscription, s/he may not have the same expertise as the previous researcher.

- Ensure they change their strategies according to the current market conditions. For example, 5 years ago ADRs (U.S. listed stocks of foreign countries) perform better than the current 5 years.

- Few if any use real money for their portfolios, as they cannot cheat with real money. That's why you never achieve the compatible performance by following what the portfolio trades if they do not use real money. Do not trust any performance claims even from reputable monitor services unless the portfolios are in real money or can be verified.

  Some sample portfolios trade excessively and they may not fit your investment strategy not to mention the broker commissions.

- When a subscription service has several strategies (say 10 for illustration), it will advertise the best returns of its top strategies (say 2 in our example) for a specific time period.

Contrary to not recommending investment services, here are very low priced or even free subscription services. By opening a small account with a broker, you can access their research. Check your current broker's website on evaluating stocks. AAII is a low-priced subscription with on-line stock research (Chapter 99). Yahoo!Finance is very popular among investors. Seeking Alpha is a good web site.

Afterthoughts

- My friend told me he saw an ad that would show him how to make $500 a day for working a few minutes before the market opens. He is nice enough to share his 'discovery' with me. If it is for real, I would be the first one to sign up. If it really works, it will not work very soon. When a strategy is over-used, it will not work. Unfortunately, a fool is born every minute as the same ad has been there for a long time.

- Currently I spend about $1,500 for all subscription services. I believe $200-$600 should cover the basic. To start, you can use your broker's web site for tools. Some have a lot of research for evaluating stocks and some even include searches. Try the biggest broker's research as they spend more on this area. Even if you do not trade with them, use their research by opening an account with the minimum balance.

- If the offer is too good to be true (like making $500 every day with little effort and little investing money), it probably is not. If they give you a free 50" TV for spending $299, most likely it is a trap with bait. Remember there is no free lunch.

  However, some bait is good like the free 30-day trial offer for an investment service or the free dinners I attended seminars on estate planning. It is part of the business cost. If I do not attend more than two dinners, eventually I would end up paying two free dinners for someone I do not even know. This book could be the best deal for your entire investment life if you invest time to read it, digest it and use the ideas that are applicable to you and the current market.

- How to monitor the recent performance of a subscription service.

  Do not trust their claims and the past performance may not have anything to do with the current or future performance unless they are from reliable sources.

  Most subscription services have a free 30-day trial offer. Take advantage of it. Before you sign up, ensure you have enough time to test it out. If you do not have time, you can sign up again using your brother-in-law's name.

To illustrate how to monitor their recent performance, if they give you 20 stocks every week, save the prices and check their performance in the same period you usually hold the stocks. It has busted many well-advertised and very popular subscription services. I prefer to compare the performance to S&P 500 index. It is better to compare it both in an up market and a down market as some strategies amplify their performance by selecting riskier stocks.

- One advertises the technique of using covered calls achieving 48% a year. I have seen these 'techniques' many times before such as "Making big money in the first 15 minutes before the opening bell". First I have strong doubt on the claim – it would drive all mutual funds out-of-business. Even it were true, it will be over-used and will not be effective. Do not waste your time and money unless you believe in fairy tales.

- There is one among hundreds of 'highly profitable' subscription I receive. Its rocket strategy can help you to move $500 to $500,000 in six months. I must be stupid not to subscribe their service. They told you how. Of course, they did not use real money in their portfolio. I could if I just selected the big winners (after the fact) and did not tell you my losers. Again, it is that great, they must be stupid to share it with me.

- On 5/2013, I received an ad boasting how great its portfolio performs from a well-known paper on investing. The cumulative return from 2001 to today is an impressive 308% beating the S&P 500's 43%. However, if you analyze it, most of the big gains are made before 2009.

  To prove it, I used their data and input their returns from 2009 to today. Their accumulative return is 37% while the S&P 500 is 66%. The more current data has better predicative power than the older data.

  The moral of the story:

  1. Read any claim with skepticism.

2. The recent performance has better predictive power than the older data.
3. When a strategy is over-used, it will become less effective.
4. The market conditions change. Some strategies work better than others in different conditions.
5. Most likely their return includes dividends while the S&P 500 index does not.
6. Test it yourself than listen from others' claims.

#Filler

How celebrities and/or newsletter owners make money for themselves

To illustrate, a TV or talk host and his staffs know what stocks they want to promote in the next show. They may have bought these stocks before the show (legal?). The viewers or listeners follow the recommendations to move the prices up. In two or three months later, these insiders dump the stocks and the stock prices come down.

I bet the recommended stocks usually follow this pattern.

Real joke

My six-year old grandson called the library about the availability of the book Mine Craft. The lady told him that only Mine Craft for Dummies was available. He told her it was not for him as he was not a dummy.

My dumb thoughts after a few laughs over his honesty:

From the eyes of a dummy (that's me), the dummy thinks he is not a dummy most likely is no dummy. However, if the dummy argues he is not a dummy solely due to his young age and naively dumb is a dummy (arguable).

I feel the word dummy has just been over-used by dummies like me. Right?

Performance magazines / newsletters

My performances in stocks selected via investing magazines and newsletters vary. However, I bet most of my successes are the result of my further evaluations.

The following uses the actual selections from Barron's Round Table in 1/8/2016. They are well-known fund managers. The result is based on 7/7/2016 (this article is written on 7/8/2016). All returns are annualized without including dividends. I compare them to SPY without including dividends. For simplicity, I exclude companies listed in foreign exchanges, currency trades and shorts.

Picks by	Annualized Returns
SPY for comparison	18.5%
Black	-12%
Cohen	-8%
Gabelli	25%
Gundlach	20%
Priest	-17%
Roger	22%
Schafer	23%
Witmer	-5%
All	8.9%

The average is almost 50% worse than the market (represented by SPY). It could be the first half of 2016 is not good for stock pickers but I will not follow these gurus blindly. I hope Barron's will publish the past returns for the last 5 years. MYL is the only stock that has been selected by more than one manager and it has an annualized loss of 23%; I treated it as one stock. I'm not responsible for any error and/or misinterpretation. The picks are based on Barron's published on June 13, 2016.

6 Hedge fund 101

LTCM, with two Nobel-prize winners, best supporting team and best technologies then, ran their hedge funds into the ground. Many hedge funds are closed due to frauds and/or poor performances.

The primary purpose is supposed to 'hedge' your investments from market plunges / dips. Since 2008, the government prints so much money, the market recovers and makes the hedges (shorts, derivatives, etc.) unnecessary. In reality, most hedge funds do not hedge.

Hedge funds get tons of press coverage as the Holy Grail of investing. The media need the advertising from this $2.5 trillion industry. It is similar to a mutual fund but most tend to take more risk for better returns. Most require higher minimum investments and more restrictions (such as longer periods to withdraw the funds).

It could be the worst deal (but best deal to the hedge funds): 2% average up front and 20% average on your profit. It is more acceptable to me if the 20% is on profit over the S&P 500 or any relevant yardstick to the specific hedge fund.

Well, if they make a lot of money for you, it is not too much to ask for. However, most risk your money by betting big recklessly. When they win, they get 20% of your profit and they use you for advertising to lure other suckers. When they lose *your* money, they do not lose a penny. It encourages them to take big risks. I do not know any hedge fund (HF) manager who pays you back your losses.

An average mutual fund charges about 1.5% management fees. An average hedge fund charges 2% that would cover the expenses to run an office, market the products and research expenses. While the average mutual fund tries to beat S&P500 index or an index specific to the fund. The real compensation of hedge fund depends on the 20% of the profit.

You have better return by investing in a no-load index fund or a diversified ETF than an average hedge fund. To calculate the average hedge fund performance, you need to include the many hedge funds that are out of business.

After a hedge fund has failed, most fund managers just open another hedge fund (if they do not go to jail due to frauds) and give you all the excuse for losing your hard-earned money. Some lose their reputation but you need to check them out.

In 2011, the hedge fund industry did not beat the S&P 500 index fund after fees. I bet the hedge fund industry did not beat the market after 2011.

Some hedge fund managers learn modern portfolio theories from Ivy League universities and apply them in the hedge funds. Often their theories are wrong due to wrong testing procedures or they cannot be sustained in real life. Many invest into their own hedge fund. It appears good at the first sight, but it is really bad for them when the fund does not perform.

They usually invest in new companies and small companies where they can have big profits swing. They need to learn the business of the company they plan to buy the stocks, interview the owners, read between the lines, and double check whether the owners are telling the truth by talking to their competitors, vendors and customers. It explains the high cost of their research. For us, we just look at the transaction of the insiders to have the better research almost instantly with a low-cost subscription service. No need travel unless you want to.

Some use their specialty in certain sectors and that's fine. If they use derivatives, be careful and that's what resulted in our 2007 financial crisis. Derivatives could reduce the risk of the portfolio if they are properly used. If you still want to invest in them, ask for their methods and their historical performance. Very few hedge funds are good. When you find a good hedge fund, most likely it has been closed to new investors or its fees are outrageous.

The owner of a famous baseball franchise lost big money from a hedge fund that concentrated in the oil sector. Almost every ETF in this sector made good money that year. He still stayed with the hedge fund and had similar miserable return the following year. I did not blame his first mistake, but on his sticking with the same hedge fund after a losing year. It could be the hedge fund gave him a hard time to take your money out.

One hedge fund has a performance of 25% every year for a long period. The SEC, take notes and investigate whether they were using insiders' info. There are very few hedge funds with consistent performance beating the market after fees. If you find some, stay with them forever.

In 1980, this industry started with really capable fund managers and made good money for their clients. After that, every analyst wanted to open a hedge fund and most did not even beat the market after their expensive fees. Alternatively, just buy the ETF SPY and relax, instead of waiting for the hedge fund to wipe out your savings. This industry is not properly regulated.

Do not believe in any articles / ads praising how great the hedge fund is without knowing their credibility and their hidden agenda. The hedge fund indexes usually ignore the survivor bias of the bankrupted hedge funds and the early exits of many hedge funds.

Since the hedge funds very seldom keep the stocks more than a year, their capital gains would be short-term and hence would be taxed at higher rates than the long-term capital gains. In addition, most funds have 1-3 year lock-up periods and only allow withdrawals on the first day of each fiscal quarter.

Afterthoughts

- From WSJ, from 1999-2008, the hedge fund industry beats the S&P 500 by 13% a year. From WSJ, from 2009 thru July 2012, it lagged the market by almost 8%.

  In 2011, the average hedge fund lost money when the S&P 500 was flat. In 2012, the average hedge fund earned about 6% when the S&P 500 was up 13%. It is a 'genius' to buy an ETF representing the entire market instead a hedge fund.

- Now hedge funds can advertise.
  A pig wearing lipstick is still a pig. If you run 5 hedge funds, you will advertise your best fund. Advertising industry will benefit and eventually their investors in hedge funds will pay for this expense.

  http://finance.fortune.cnn.com/2013/07/10/sec-votes-to-let-hedge-funds-advertise/?iid=HP_River

- A hedge fund article from SA.
  http://seekingalpha.com/article/584861-hedge-funds-are-they-just-smooth-operators?source=kizur

- Another hedge fund fraud.
  http://money.cnn.com/2013/07/25/investing/sac-capital-charges/index.html?iid=HP_LN

- Gold even managed by great hedge fund manager is down as of 7/2013.
  http://www.cnbc.com/id/100855708

- A famous hedge fund manager (so is the one on Sears) has big losses in JCP and shorting another company. It teaches us to diversify and be conservative.
  http://money.cnn.com/2013/08/26/investing/bill-ackman-sells-jcpenney/index.html?iid=HP_River

- Hedge funds must have a hard time in 2013. Hedging against a rising market is a fool's game.

- The average expense for mutual funds is 2% and it is probably more if you consider other fees such as trade commissions. In 50 years, the $10,000 investment will grow to $1,170,000 assuming a 10% return a year. However, about $700,000 will be the cost of the typical mutual fund. It will be better to buy an ETF (far lower fee) and avoid market plunges described in this book.

Links
Modern Portfolio Theory:
http://tonyp4idea.blogspot.com/2012/05/modern-portfolio-theories.html

LTCM:https://en.wikipedia.org/wiki/LongTerm_Capital_Management

Hedge Fund: http://en.wikipedia.org/wiki/Hedge_fund

7 No investor heroes

As of 1/2012, Bill Miller is stepping down after big recent losses. Buffett's last three year performance is so lousy that he should be ashamed and should not show his handsome face in public (too harsh on him but we all enjoy to make fun of winners). Gross, the king of bonds, made serious mistakes, so was Whitney on muni bonds (though she should be right on longer term; she learned the lesson not fighting against the city hall).

It was same for a very famous shorter of Netflix with convincing arguments. Their arguments were correct but the timing was not. The fund manager of the decade in a famous financial service advocated bank stocks in 2007. He was burned badly and you would too if you followed him.

There are many examples of heroes turning into disgrace in the past. Recently my local newspaper Boston Globe had an article stating most top fund managers did not beat the S&P 500 index last year. Even Professor Irvin Fisher, the father of Wall Street, did not predict the 1929 crash and lost a bundle including most of his own life savings.

Recently Barron's had a round table discussion on 2012 market with the top experts. They also listed the recommended stocks from these experts a year ago and their performances. Guess what? Their average did not even beat the Dow index. Was I stupid enough to follow their 2012 recommendations?

At least, most did not publish their past performances in the beginning of 2013 if they under performed. Most are not good pickers or their strategies do not work this time. That's why I preach to monitor your current strategies.

We learn:

- Retire at your peak like Peter Lynch. You can call him a coward but he has a good sleep and laughs all the way to the bank. With his fame, it is easy to sell some books and live nicely and respectably.

- Do not invest on your losing horse like Miller. Doubling on the way down without good reason is a fool's game and it could be the last straw that terminates his brilliant career. When he won all the time, he did not expect that he was wrong this time. Success could blind our eyes and give us false security.

  Bill Miller has beaten the market index 12 times in a row. Peter Lynch was the premier fund manager. The two and many similar outstanding fund managers have to retire earlier due to poor performance, deteriorating performance, or smart enough to realize that s/he cannot beat the market consistently in the long run.

  Lessons are:
  - Using the previous performance of any fund manager to invest in a fund could be dangerous to your financial health.

  - Prefer to follow funds that have above average returns for five years (ensure the same fund manager).

  - May beat the market by investing in ETFs and using market timing described in this book.

- Need specialty advice on banks, bio drugs and mines. Their financial statements do not tell the whole story. Avoid them unless you feel this selected sector is moving up and/or you really understand these sectors. Use ETFs and mutual funds for these sectors as they spread out the risk and/or they have experts in selected sectors.

- Is your loser stock a good deal now when it loses half of its value? Usually not. Should someone be excited when the dividend yield is doubled due to the loss of half of its stock value? Definitely not. Do your own intelligent research. A fool and his money are soon parted.

- Do not believe you're always right all the time and put all your eggs in a basket. Market is irrational as it is created by irrational folks. The black swan could occur unexpectedly. The one who made millions with all his money in one deal is just lucky or using insider's information. Diversify and play it safe. I never bet my entire farm on any one of my predictions even though they have been right more often than wrong.

- Even the genius could not be right all the time. It only takes one big loss to wipe out your entire savings if you bet it all. Except for our ex-President Bush, we should treat investment as going to battle with an exit plan to reduce your losses.

- Gambling with other folks' money is better than with your own. The most you lose is your job, but not your life-time savings and the bonuses in good times.

- Quit at the peak. We still remember the beautiful face of Princess D forever, don't we?

Afterthoughts

- We do have some great stock pickers and I am following them but checking their performance from time to time. Einhorn is well known (though his portfolio is slipping). Google 'Einhorn' to check his current picks.

  Einhorn is a great investor, but he has made many mistakes too such as betting on gold in 6/2013.

  Arne Alsin is not well known. Click here for his performance.
  I was told another smart stock picker is Michael Larson and he manages investment for Bill Gates.

Links

Buffett. http://tonyp4idea.blogspot.com/2011/06/mr-buffett.html
Irvin Fisher. https://en.wikipedia.org/wiki/Irving_Fisher
Einhorn.http://en.wikipedia.org/wiki/David_Einhorn_%28hedge_fund_manager%29
http://www.cnbc.com/id/100855708
Arne Alsin. http://seekingalpha.com/author/arne-alsin
Michael Larson.
http://en.wikipedia.org/wiki/Michael_Larson_%28businessman%29

8 2011, the year stock pickers died

2011 is a year when stock pickers (particularly the value pickers) did not perform. The performances of AAII screens and the mutual funds confirm it. Most investment advisers / newsletters did not beat the market index in 2011. Check the performances of your investment newsletters such as Value Line and IBD. However, do not give them up. They may not perform for a short while but they will return back to the normal performance and hopefully sooner.

Most likely it is due to the excessive printing of money. The market was volatile with most of the gains in the first half of the year of 2011. Traders using technical analysis did better than the stock pickers based on fundamentals as they reacted to the trends.

From my limited data of about 250 stocks for a period of about half a year, I tested out which fundamentals do not work well in predictability in 2011. They are analysts' grade (Fidelity's summary grade of analysts for a specific stock), cash flow and the short %. Normally, the stocks with analysts' grade A (or above 8 from Fidelity's Advisor Opinions), cash flow (grade A from Blue Chip Growth) and shorter % (less than 5) would perform better than the average. Not this time. You can obtain most of these mentioned metrics from many other sources and most likely reach the same conclusion.

I'm adjusting my search criteria accordingly for swing trades. I'm not buying a lot and waiting for the big dip that I expect it will come. However, when I see bargains, I'll buy them and wait for these stocks to recover.

My suggestion

Your fundamental metrics need to be checked whether they still perform in the current market. When they worked a year ago, it does not mean they still work today.

Links

Stock pickers: http://www.tonyp4idea.blogspot.com/2011/11/no-more-investing-hero.html

9 This time is different

Today is really different.

Recently I read a classic book on investing. Similar to most other classic books, most ideas are not applicable to today's market. The author died more than 50 years ago. By my rough estimate, the ideas are 30% correct and 30% incorrect. The remaining fall into the grey area that they are only correct in specific market conditions and/or specific interpretations. Most correct ideas are now conventional wisdom and most likely they have been repeated in this book. The incorrect ideas are described as follows.

- Most of these books described strategies in investing and then selected examples to fit the strategies. Most of my examples are from my personal experience. My bad experience could be more beneficial to you by not repeating the same error.

- Tax laws have been changed since then. Roth IRA could be the best thing since slice bread if you're eligible. Check Tax Avoidance chapter. This book has a link to the current tax law from Wikipedia to keep you updated with the current and future tax laws. Your tax lawyer or accountant is no substitution.

- Today most brokers' commission rates are so low that it makes some trading strategies more effective than before. My commission rate is $5 per trade (after some negotiation on frequent trading) and one account is even commission-free for a year via a special promotion. Your Dad may have paid over $300 for commission per trade.

- Your Dad did not have Technical Analysis. I use it effectively to detect market plunges. Many good technicians make great money.

- Tracking 'mispriced stocks' is less useful today than 50 years ago. Today these stocks are screened every day by investment subscriptions, fund managers and even retail investors. The extensively used P/E is only one metric among many to determine the value of a stock.

The only reason I can think of why the stocks are mispriced is via over-reaction by the media and manipulation. The media exaggerate in order to sell their viewership and most information is outdated.

Most 'experts' from the financial TVs manipulate the public in order for them to buy or sell specific stocks to their advantages. If you cannot turn off these TV or radio programs, analyze what they preach. Sometimes you act opposite to what they say and make a profit. To prove my point, check out what they say and see whether it is correct in 6 months. Usually their predictions are correct in the first few weeks and it could be due to my herd **theory**.

Goldman Sacks is one manipulator to me. A famous former fund manager advised folks to buy a specific stock while unloading it and he did not go to jail.

Today, the real 'mispriced' stocks could be those who are losing the competitive edge of their major products, using high debts to boost up the earnings, having major lawsuits pending, etc. It only happens when the entire market is on sale.

Note. Although most financial ratios can be displayed easily (try finviz.com), I still recommend check out the most updated financial statements of a company you want to evaluate it deeper.

- Retail investors have most of the financial information of a company and the economy at the same instance as the Wall Street experts. Actually we have more advantages. Our PCs are fast enough for our needs in evaluating investments and our spreadsheets can do most required analyses. Indicated by any abnormal large volume of a stock from trading by fund managers, day traders could take advantage of it.

- From 1970 to 2000, the market returned for an average of 10% including dividends. Market timing would likely deteriorate your return. However, since 2000, we have two major market plunges with an average loss of about 45%. Today, market timing is critical to your financial health.

- We have new regulations, which are supposed to protect investors (from insiders' trading for example). However the government intervenes in the market by pumping up too much money to cause a non-correlation of the economy and the market. It seldom happened.

  The chance of another 1987 crash is minimized with new regulations. We do not learn a lot from the 1929 crash as our market and its regulations are quite different from then.

- The economy may recover without employment recovery. Most jobs today can be outsourced. Big companies hire the best workers at the least costs in any country in the world. The world is getting smaller via better communication and more efficient transportation.

  Free trade and globalization make the world connected better and the participants should benefit. Without employment recovery, it would affect many sectors such as housing and retail. When one country is down economically, many other countries will be affected. Watching the economy of the USA alone is not enough today.

- Sir Newton and Irving Fisher lost a lot of their money in their investments, so their high IQs have nothing to do with investing. Even the Nobel-prize winners ran their hedge fund LTCM to bankruptcy. It also teaches us to diversify and the black swan could wipe out our entire savings if we bet all in one strategy or one stock.

  We have to change our strategy to adapt to the current market. The market 50 years ago most likely was not the same as the market today. Fewer lessons from 50 years ago are valuable than the lessons learned in the last 15 years.

- We do have new challenges and new tools.
  The big boys (mutual fund and pension managers) could manipulate the market. It could be a nice conspiracy theory that the blood-sucking big boys meet on the first full moon every month to determine the market direction and/or which sectors to rotate to. However, with today's internet, the big boys could

drive the market fast and violently and the retail investors would likely follow.

As high as 50% of today's trades are decided and executed by computers. When they act at the same time and in the same direction, the market would surge or plunge fiercely without warning.

High speed trading could hurt us but also could benefit us. Sector rotation, ETFs, contra ETFs, options and day trading should be examined and understood (even if you don't participate) by today's investors.

Dow Theory with emphasis on the Transport sector loses some of its luster as a lot of products do not have to be shipped by rails such as the digitized music and movies. It is similar to USPS in handling your mail.

These are the tools and strategies that your Dad's generation did not use; not to mention those books written 50 years ago that did not have to deal with our challenges.

- With today's advances in publishing, books can be published / updated with minimum effort and distributed throughout the world. There is no need to print and store large numbers of books. Books can include multi-media features and links on other articles. Readers enjoy the lower cost and larger choices. Updating today's digital business books to keep up with the current market is easy, low-cost (or even free) and efficiently done.

Conclusion
Technology and new regulations change our tools in investing. Your Daddy did not have today's powerful PCs, spreadsheets, internet, etc. The tax laws and regulation are changing every year. Read any book with an open mind and apply what works in today's market.

Links
Newton and his market loss:
http://www.cnn.com/2009/POLITICS/07/29/levenson.finance.regulation/
Irving Fisher:
http://en.wikipedia.org/wiki/Irving_Fisher
LTCM:
https://en.wikipedia.org/wiki/Long-Term_Capital_Management

10 Financial topics for retirees

This chapter describes my own experiences. Check the current tax laws and consult your tax professional on any related topic. Check my Disclaimer in the Introduction section.

Will and estate planning

They will lure you to their presentations by giving you meals at expensive restaurants. If your estate is small (such as below the Federal exemption), a simple will signed by a notary public and the assignments of beneficiaries in your broker's accounts may be sufficient.

Check the estate tax requirements in your state. Some move to another state that has favorable estate tax treatment or even give up the US citizenship. Some did not take out the life support until the following year that had larger exemption. These are extreme examples.

Many transfer their houses to their children to avoid long-term care expenses.

I had several 'free' meals before I settled for my lawyer. He put my house into a joint trust.

Taxes

I was lucky (or unlucky) to have higher tax rate in retirement than my working year due to good investment return. Hence, it would be better for me not to postpone taxes during my work years. At 70 ½, we are required to withdraw our retirement accounts (except Roth IRA in the current tax law). Before 70½, I converted some 401K into Roth IRA as allowed in the current tax law. I paid taxes but could be less at 70 ½ and/or when I annualize my Annuity. Everyone's tax situation is different.

Market Timing

From 1970-2000, the average annualized return is about 10%. Market timing may not help at all. However, since 2000, we had two market plunges (2000 and 2007) with an average loss of about 45%. Check out the chapters on Market Timing. To summarize:

- Do not invest during a market plunge.
- Invest aggressively in the early recovery phase of a market cycle as described.
- Invest conservatively during other phases with stop losses.

Make your money last

You may never run out of money if you withdraw 4% of your total asset every year. You may want to withdraw less when inflation is high and/or interest rate is low.

http://moneyover55.about.com/od/RetirementAccountWithdrawals/a/What-Is-The-4-Rule-In-Retirement.htm

Health

I highly recommend the book China Study by Dr. Campbell. In short, eat more whole grains, vegetables and fruits particularly with different colors and avoid meats / dairy products. Replace milk with soy milk. Avoid cakes, cookies and potato chips.

More information

This book concentrates on investing and it tries not to duplicate the financial topics for retirees with other well-written books. I obtained the following books in Kindle format for 99 cents each from Amazon.com. They can only make a tiny profit by selling a lot in a crowded market and/or use it as a vehicle to sell you more services / products.

Retirement Financial Planning for Baby Boomers by Whitney Smith.

Retirement Solutions: Financial Strategies for Today's Retirees by Michael Dallas, CFP.

Afterthoughts

This book concentrates on how to invest during investing. In essence, you should invest more conservatively as you cannot afford to lose money at this stage of life. I recommend:

1. Market timing on market plunges. You should exit the market earlier and reenter later to be safer. When the market is close (not exceed) the SMA-350, exit the market. Same for reentry.

2. Market timing on corrections. Allow 20% (instead of the recommended 15%) in cash. You will not catch corrections as easily as market plunges as they are harder to detect. Treat it as insurance policy.

3. Employ Tom's strategy which is very conservative.

You will sacrifice some performance with better safety. However, you should have more time in enjoying life. Unless you enjoy investing, there are plenty of things to do in life and money is not the ultimate goal.

Besides the books mentioned above, the following are some articles that are relevant to you.

Retire overseas. http://www.marketwatch.com/story/5-reasons-not-to-retire-in-the-us-2014-08-07

Managed Accounts.
http://blogs.marketwatch.com/encore/2014/08/05/managed-accounts-too-pricey-for-retirees/

Section III: Fundamental metrics

1 Mysteries of P/E

If you believe you can make good money by selecting stocks with low P/Es solely, dream on. If it were that easy, there would be no poor folks. However, buying fundamentally sound companies would reduce the risk and improve the chance of its appreciation.

P/E is the most misunderstood indicator. To me, it is the most useful one among all metrics if it is properly used. Earnings are the key to stock appreciation and P/E measures its value. To illustrate on P/E, you pay a million for a hot-dog cart in NYC. Even if its earnings increase year after year, you will never recoup your investment as you have paid too much even for a good business.

"Buy stocks with P/E below 15 and earnings positive" is not true in many cases. P/E growth (PEG) should be considered at least as a prospect of the company. Many retailers were destroyed by Amazon and many newspapers were destroyed by Facebook and Google. Which sector do you want to buy: the sector in up trending or the dying sector even with a better P/E?

Most old books on value are based on old industries that are no longer applicable in today's market. Read these books but ask the above question.

Better definition

P/E should be inverted as E/P, which is termed as Earnings Yield. Earnings Yield is easy to be compared and understood. It takes care of negative earnings for screening stocks and ranking (comparing stocks with the better P/E first). If you sort P/E in ascending order, your order will be wrong with the negative earnings but right with E/P.

It is usually compared to a 10-year Treasury bill yield (or 30 years) or a CD rate. If the stock has 5% earnings yield and your one-year CD is 1%, then it beats the CD by 4% in absolute numbers and four times better. However, the CD is virtually risk free (with deposit amount limits in most banks). Earning yield is an estimated guess and it may not materialize.

Many ways to predict E/P

- Based on the last 12 months. Project it to the Forward E/P. It is also called the last twelve month E/P.

- Based on analysts' educated guesses. Guesses may not materialize. Based on my experience, the expected usually predicts better than the one based on the last 12 months. This is the one I use most and many investing subscriptions provide this Forward P/E (same as the Expected P/E) or expected E/P.

Usually I do not trust the analyst's opinions due to their conflict of interest. However, the earnings estimate is my exception.

- Based on the last month or the last quarter. Latest information could be better for predictions. However, they are not good for seasonal businesses such as the retail where most sales are done during the Christmas season.
- Besides the Pow PE described later, I take the average of the earnings yield EY as:

The Avg. EY = (EY from the last twelve month + Expected EY + EY from the current month of prior year) / 3

It averages out using figures from the past, the present and the future. If no one has used it, I claim shamelessly it is my original idea.

Best E/P could not be the best

Very high E/P could be signs of troubles ahead such as a lawsuit pending, fraud, etc. If you find companies E/P over 50%, it means two years' profits could be equal to the entire cost of the company! I can tell you right away that they probably smell fishy unless you believe that there is a free lunch in life.

However, from time to time, some bargains do exist due to certain conditions, or the Wall Street is just wrong about the company. I found one in my year-end screen and that gave me huge return. You need to find out whether they are bargains or traps. When the E/P is low (sometimes even negative) but is improving fast, it could mean big profits for you. Fundamentalists may miss this opportunity in the early stages due to the unfavorable E/P, but it could be the most profitable time to buy. Sometimes, it could be a turnaround.

During a recession, most good companies have a hard time in promoting new products as the consumers are thrifty. At the same time, it usually is the best time to develop products if they have enough cash to finance them. In this case, there will be no alarm even with negative earnings. The only alarm is when a company cannot meet the debt obligations.

Some companies can manipulate earnings via dirty tricks in accounting. It could make this year look really good, but it is harder or even impossible to continue the same trick for many years. Check out the footnotes in the financial statement.

E/P and PEG

For value investing, E/P is usually used and the higher the better. Watch out when it is extraordinarily high.

PEG (P/E growth) measures the rate of improving P/E. '1' is supposed to be neutral to most investors. When it is below 1, it is undervalued, and vice versa.

PEG = (P/E) / Earnings Growth Rate

They have a similar problem with P/E with negative earnings.

Which of the following two stocks do you want to buy based on their historical earning yields and earnings growth?

1. A stock that has a 10% earnings yield with no earnings growth.
2. A stock that has an 8% earnings yield with 50% earnings growth.

If the earnings growth continues, in next year the second stock should pay 12%, substantially better than the first stock. This is another reason we should use forward earnings rather than historical earnings.

PEG may give a low value for companies that pay high dividends. To correct it,

PEG = (P/E)/ (Earning Growth Rate + Dividend Yield)

When the general market favors growth stocks, weigh more on growth metrics including PEG. I claim no credit on the adjusted PEG.

Fundamental metrics

E/P is one of the metrics you should use but not exclusively. If the earning yield is high but the % of debt is high too, then a good bargain may not be as good as it appears to be.

Some other metrics may not be easily found in the financial statements such as the intangibles, insider buying, pension obligations, trade secrets, losing market share, brand name, customers' loyalty, etc. It is interesting that most metrics change its ability to predict from time to time.

P/E variations

There are other P/E variations like Shiller P/E (same as CAPE and PE10). Shiller P/E can also be used to track the current market valuation. It is controversial and its value is easily misinterpreted. Hence, use it as a reference only unless you understand all its issues. I prefer to use two year average of the P/E instead of 10 as I believe the market changes too much over a ten year span. Currently Shill P/E does not work that well as before. It is due to the excessive printing of money.

Compare a company's current P/E to its average P/E in the last 5 years. Also compare it to the average value of the companies in the same industry. The average P/E for high-tech companies is different from supermarkets for example. They are available from Fidelity.

P/E is more reliable for a group of stocks (SPY for example) instead of individual stocks which have too many other metrics and intangibles to deal with. When you compare the total return of an ETF to a corresponding index, you need to add the respective dividends to the index to ensure a fair comparison of total returns. As of this writing, the S&P 500 is paying about a 2% dividend.

EV/EBITDA is another way to measure the value of a company. This metric has its advantages and disadvantages over P/E. It includes other important data such as cash and debt. EBITDA/EV is equivalent to E/P including other mentioned metrics. I prefer to use it over E/P. Some sites do not provide it if the earnings is negative. The disadvantage to me is it does not use expected earnings. This ratio can be found under Yahoo!Finance.

Garbage in, garbage out

I do not trust most financial statements from emerging countries, especially the smaller companies. Watch out for fraudulent data. Most metrics can be manipulated. Recently I have a US stock that lost 18% in one day due to the SEC's investigation of its financial data.

The announced earnings may not be reflected in the financial statements that you use from the web. Ensure your data is up-to-date by checking the date of the financial statements. Seeking Alpha has transcripts for the earnings announcements that would save you a trip to attend the companies' quarterly meetings.

Sector and entire market

You can find the value of a sector using the P/E of an ETF for that sector. It is similar for the market. For example, use SPY (an ETF simulating the S&P 500 index). If it is lower than the average (15 to me), then most likely the market is good value and a buy signal. It is one of the many hints for market timing.

Where to use P/E

Each highlight of the following corresponds to one of my books. Click it for the description of the strategy.

My book on top-down approach starts with a safe market, then sector analysis, fundamental analysis, intangible analysis and optionally technical analysis. P/E is one of the many metrics in fundamental analysis.

There are many styles of investing. In general, fundamental analysis is important when you hold the stock longer.

- P/E is important in Long-Term Swing, Dividend Investing, Retirees and Conservative Strategies.
- My max value is 20 and 25 for tech companies. I ignore it if they have high potential for appreciation that could be indicated by insider purchases. However, many unknown companies then had a P/E over 50. Tesla had a P/E over 1,000 at one time.
- P/E is moderately important in Short-Term Swing and Sector Rotation.
- P/E is the least important in Momentum Strategy and Day Trading.

Summary

Again, one metric should not dictate the reason to trade a stock. Compare the company P/E to its industry average and its own five-year average. In addition, many industries have cycles. If you buy it at the peak of the industry, the P/E may mislead you. Besides fundamental analysis, you need to consider intangible analysis and time the entry / exit point by using technical analysis. Intangible analysis evaluates information that cannot be summarized into numeric metrics such as a lawsuit pending.

True P/E

"EV/EBITDA" is available from Yahoo!Finance and other sources. The true EY is "1/Ture PE". I call it "True" for the lack of a better term as it represents the financial situation of the company better. This could be the most important metric for many.

Earnings can be manipulated. For example, the company management can lower the P/E ratio by buying back its stocks. In this case the earnings per share is boosted but in reality there is no change in the company's financial fundamentals. The true P/E takes into consideration the reduced cash. EBITBA stands for "Earnings Before Interest, Taxes, Depreciation, and Amortization".

Be careful when EV or "EBITDA" is negative. Most likely you should avoid the stocks with a negative EV.

Yahoo!Finance usually leaves EV/EVITDA blank for financial institutions such banks, loan companies and REITS. In this case, use forward earnings yield (= 1 / Forward P/E or Pow Earnings Yield described next.

Pow P/E

You should use the described "EV/EBITDA" and hence "Pow P/E" can be ignored. There are some cases that Pow P/E is better: 1. "EV/EBITDA" may not be available for reasons such as negative asset and 2. Use of Forward Earnings instead of Earnings based on the last twelve months. The following is an exercise on how I simulate it from Finviz.com with metrics that are readily available.

I modified P/E to take care of cash and debts. I use my last name due to being easier to distinguish from P/E and it has nothing to do with my ego.

Pow P/E = (P - Cash per Share + Debt per Share) / (Earning - Interest gained per share - Interest paid per share)

Pow Earnings Yield = 1 / Pow P/E

Here is a comparison of E/P (Earnings Yield), Expected Earnings Yield (Forward E /P), True Yield (EBITD/EV) and Pow Earning Yields, which is based one Forward (Expected) Earnings as of 10/14/2021.

	CARS	MPAA
Earnings Yield	1%	7%
Expected Earnings Yield	12%	12%
True Yield	13%	11%
Pow Earnings Yield	5%	9%

P/E is not always important

The following is my test from 1/2/2020 to 10/14/2020. RSP is similar to SPY except that the stocks in the S&P 500 index are equally weighed. EY (= E/P) is Expected Earnings Yield and there is no stocks with EY less than 0. DY is Dividend Yield. GPE is the growth of P/E. As in my book, I use annualized returns and dividends are not included. This test does not mean a lot, but it tells us what these metrics behave during this period, or it indicates **Value is not a good metric in this period**, and it may indicate momentum is better in this period. Most big winners start as small companies with **high P/E** (from 30 to 100). Many of them have important technologies or special systems that would change the world such as Microsoft, Facebook, Amazon and Walmart to name a few. Their sales have increased substantially year after year.

Examples of not depending on low P/Es. Before the financial crisis in 2008, P/Es of most bank stocks had 10-year low. After they announced the earnings, P/Es of many of them surged to over 100 and the stock prices suffered losses of more than 80% within 12 months. The stock price of Bethlehem Steel with P/E of 2 at one time went to zero. Need to find out why the stock is so cheap via intangible analysis and qualitative analysis.

The following is very rough testing and there are many limitations in the database. However, the conclusion is quite convincing to me and some are opposite to the contrary beliefs. For example, I expected the higher EY the better, but not in this test.

	Ann. Return	Indicator	Comment
RSP 500 All	-2%		
EY (top 10)	-54%	Bad	Contrary
GPE (top 10)	-20%	Bad	Contrary
Select All or top 100.			
DY = 0	16%	Good	
DY (top 100)	-19%	Bad	
DY / 1 and 2	2%		
EY 3 to 4	15%	Good	Second best
EY 2 to 3	6%	Good	Third best
EY 1 to 2	31%	Good	Best
EY 0 to 1	-39%	Bad`	

I use some metrics from a service I subscribe to that are not included here. Two major metrics of this subscription have a return of around 20%. Most subscriptions including the free Fidelity (to some extent) give you three composite scores: Total, Fundamental and Timing. I wish to check out the recent predictability of Fidelity's Equity Summary Score if they have a historical database. Most of them take out the delisted and /or bankrupt companies in their databases.
Link: P/E: https://www.youtube.com/watch?v=4KkTGx2bK_4

2 *Fundamental metrics*

ROE

Return of equity (ROE = Net Income / Equity) could be the most important financial indicator to determine how well the management is doing their job. However, in recent years, this metric has been overused and loses its prediction reliability.

The company's return on equity for at least the last five years would indicate how the stock price endures major financial downturns as well as upturns.

Comparing the ROE to the average ROE for the sector is a good indicator on how well the company is managed compared to its peers. Some sectors including utilities have low average ROEs.

Market Cap (Capitalization)

Market Cap = Total no. of outstanding shares * share price

I recommend the beginners buy U.S. stocks with a market cap greater than 800 M (million). Here are the current conventions (everyone's convention is different) and they should be adjusted to inflation.

Class	Market Cap (million)
Nano Cap	< $50M
Micro Cap	$50M to $250M
Small Cap	$250M to $1B (billion)
Mid Cap	$1B to $10B
Large Cap (Blue Chip)	$10B to $50B
Mega Cap	>50B

The higher the cap is, usually the less risky the stock would be. Nano Cap and Micro Cap are reserved for speculators or owners of the companies. Small Cap and Mid Cap are for knowledgeable investors as most institutional investors would skip these stocks in these caps especially Small Cap. Large Cap, Mega Cap and some Mid Cap are the stocks traded by institutional investors. They are thoroughly researched continuously.

My metrics

My current favorites are Forward P/E, PEG, Fidelity's Equity Summary Score, Short % of outstanding shares, Free Cash Flow, ROE and Debt Load / Equity.

In addition, I use many summarized metrics from different sources. For example, one of my subscription services gives me a composite rank for fundamentals and another one for momentum. To illustrate, click here for Blue Chip Growth which is no longer free for stock analysis. Enter IBM as the stock symbol. As of 2/2013, it gives

C for a Total Grade, D for Quantity Grade and B for Fundamental Grade. The Total Grade is usually a composite grade of other grades.

Use the metrics to screen through the stocks to reduce the number of stocks for further consideration.

Mid, high and low values of common metrics

Metric	Mid Range	Low Range	High Range
P/E (last 12 months)	< 10	>40	< 4
Price / Cash Flow	< 12	>30	< 4
Price / Sales	< 2.5	>3	< .2
Price / Book	< 2.0	>4	< .2
PEG	< 1.5	>2	< .2

High Range means good values (although in this table it means low numbers), but sometimes it is too good to be true. Low Range means bad values. To illustrate, many internet stocks in 2000 had P/E over 40 (bad) while a neglected bargain stock has a P/E of 3 (supposed to be good). A bargain could also mean they could have some hidden problems. In reality, I prefer the Mid Range. Using P/E to illustrate, it should be between 4 and 10. Adjust the range according to your personal tolerance and the current market conditions. If the market trend is up, you may want to relax the range to 5 to 12 for example otherwise you cannot find too many stocks for further evaluation.

These values are my selections based on data for about 10 years. They are used for predicting the performance of a stock in a year; review the ranges every 6 months in the current market.

The metrics with the high-range and mid-range values offer better predictions for the stock price appreciation. From the above table, the stocks with the low-range values have a better chance than other stocks to lose money in a year or so. Some favorable numbers could be high values instead of low values such as ROE.

However, the range values could change. When the market favors momentum or you do not keep stocks for less than a month or so, the momentum metrics including PEG and price growth could be better predictors. We need to check to see whether the current market favors which metrics: Value or Growth – some websites and subscription services identify the current favorite. In addition, the performance of each metric should be evaluated every 3 to 6 months. In addition, new range values need to be adjusted with the above table.

Fundamental metrics take a longer time (about 6-12 months vs. 1 month for momentum metrics) for the performance to materialize. The metrics in the above table besides PEG are all fundamental metrics. Except for financial stocks, P/B is always worthless.

Examples of searching with high range values

Stocks with low-range values for most metrics (such as 40 in P/E in the above table) could be risky. Hence, select the stocks with the mid-range value (e.g. 10 for P/E). Avoid the low-range values indicated by the metrics.

Here is one example of selecting stocks with high range values of P/E and P/B. Most likely, you will not find too many stocks with these criteria.

E > 0 and
P/E < 4 and
P/B < .2

E is earning per share and we need the company to be profitable.

High range values could indicate something is wrong with the company, e.g. a lawsuit pending. I would consider a P/E of less than 4 is suspicious. However, very small companies are often neglected by the market, so they could be solid companies. Don't forget to do your due diligence and spend more time in thoroughly evaluating the stock and its industry.

The stocks with the low-range values have a greater chance of losing money in the next year or so. That is proven statistically as a group despite some exceptions. AMZN[2] is not a valued stock by its high P/E or its high P/B. However, if the company is investing for the future by building infrastructure and capturing the market share, you may ignore these unfavorable metrics. Personally I prefer fundamentally sound companies today.

Note. P/B is not a good metric for established companies and / or companies with a lot of research such as IBM. Many metric formulae are outdated due to ignoring intellectual properties, patents and market appeals such as brand names.

Example of a search for mid-range values

E > 0 and
P/E < 10 and
P/E > 4

In this case, you only include companies with positive earnings and P/Es within the range from 4 to 10 exclusively. You should find many companies with the mid-range values of P/Es.

Add other filters such as minimum price, market cap and average volume. If you do not find too many stocks, relax your criteria (start with mid-range values in the table), and vice versa to limit the number of stocks. If you usually find stocks with a screen but not today, it usually means that the market is overvalued and that you cannot find many bargain stocks.

Again, it is the first step to narrow down the number of stocks to be analyzed. Your metrics will not cover stocks with special situations. For example, IBM always has had a high Price/Book value for as long as I can remember and therefore it does not mean it should be excluded.

The searches based on fundamental metrics help us to narrow stocks for further evaluation. Occasionally I abandon the scoring system for some stocks under special conditions.

Compare a company's metrics to its sector's averages
This could be the most powerful comparison: Compare Apples to Apples.

You may want to compare the metrics of a company to the averages of that sector. The average of supermarket's P/S is extremely low and hence it has no meaning to compare a supermarket's P/S to most other sectors. Some sectors like utilities need high debt to run a utility company.

However, when the average P/E or other metric of a sector is suddenly lower than its historical average, it could mean that sector is out-of-favor and/or the sector is having a better value.

This following table compares Apple to its sector and a retail sector on a specific date for illustration. All the metrics will change.

Metric	Apple	Computer	Retail
P/E	11	19	24
(5 year average)	16	17	15
PEG	.6	N/A	1.4
Price /Cash Flow	9.4	8.1	9.2
Price /Book	3.3	3.0	3.6
EPS Growth	-6%	-42%	2.6%
(last 5 years)	62%	45%	11%
Operating Margin	20%	15%	8%
ROE	30%	14%	19%
Debt / Equity	2%	7%	88%
Inventory Turnover	76%	53%	4.55x

From the above table, some metrics only make sense for an industrial sector (Computer for Apple). In this case, you may want to compare AAPL to Computer, and not to Retail.

"Debt / Equity" indicates that the retail sector needs to borrow more than the computer sector for example. Of course retail stores has high Inventory Turnover.

Top down approach

First, compare whether the market is risky. Second, select the best sector; there are many sites including Finviz.com to select the best sector. Then compare the fundamental metrics of the major stocks within that sector.

Some metrics do not apply

Using financial institutions as an example, usually P/B is more useful than P/CF. However, the quality of a loan (not a metric here) is more important than all metrics as we found out in 2007. P/S is more important for retails. However, the expected P/E is most important for most other sectors.

When you believe a sector is the currently best (a criterion available in many screeners), select the best stocks in this sector.

Compare metrics to its five-year average

If the company's five-year average of P/E (available from Fidelity and many other sites) is 20 and today it is 10. It is 100% under-valued by this standard. Also, you may want to try other metrics such as debt/equity and compare it to the five-year average.

Growth Metrics

The growth metrics are growth rates of the stock price, sales, earnings, etc. They are useful for growth investors.

Even for value investors, the earnings growth rate is very important, as most stocks with substantial gains have increased their earnings growth first. If the earnings has grown but the price remains the same (i.e. PEG), then the potential for price appreciation will be higher and most likely it will return to the historical average P/E.

Momentum Metrics

Momentum metrics is part of growth. The rates of increase of the stock price, the volume… are the major metrics. Earnings revision is another one especially in earnings announcement seasons (usually 4 times a year).

Fidelity and many subscription services provide a composite rank with name Timely or similar name. The following could be part of this Timely score: SMA-50, Q-Q sales increase and recent price appreciation. In my momentum portfolio, I use these metrics and ignore all the other metrics as my average holding period is less than 30 days for momentum strategies.

Insiders' buying

Insiders sell their stocks for many reasons. When insiders buy a lot of their companies' stocks at market prices, take notice. Insiders know better than anyone about the health of their companies and their industries.

Select Insiders' purchases from one of the available sites such as Finviz.com. Ignore the option exercises. I prefer the high ratios of Net Total Purchase Value / Market Cap and the purchases by more than one insider. Be careful that the insiders purchase the stocks after selling a similar amount of stock in a brief time span.

OpenInsider is a good site for this info.
InsiderSights is a good one too with more capable tools that would take more time to learn.

Where to get the metrics
You can get this information from the website with no or low cost such as Finviz.com, your broker's site, AAII (very low cost) and Fidelity.

The following subscriptions are at a little higher cost but they are still less than $1,000 per year: Value Line, IBD, Zacks, VectorVest and Stock Screen 123. Many data from different vendors are duplicated such as P/E. You will save time by concentrating on one or two sources.

Many vendors provide a composite metric such as a value metric to cover P/E, debt… and a timing metric to cover Technical Analysis indicators, PEG, price appreciation rate…

Short % is a useful metric available in Finviz.com. For Fidelity customers, you can click on Research and then Stock. Enter the stock name, and then click on Detailed. I find Fidelity's Analysts' Opinions quite useful.

Finviz.com provides a lot of useful information free of charge. It also provides a screen function. The 'Help' button describes Finviz's functions and all the metrics monitored.

Other sources are: Insider Cow, NASDAQ Guru Analysis ...

Monitor the recent performance of the metrics
The predictability of most metrics has proven not to perform consistently as many investors and fund managers found out. My theory is that the specific metric works better in some market conditions than others. To test which ones work better currently, check their performance in the last three months and use those that perform well. This is what my scoring system in the book Scoring Stocks is based on.

Why some metrics fail sometimes

Most investors are using metrics to screen stocks, but few are successful consistently. Some investment companies have top analysts dedicated to projects looking for the right strategy. My guesses why they fail are:

1. Metrics need to be monitored to see its effectiveness on current market conditions.

2. Besides fundamental metrics, there are many intangibles.

3. When they have too many followers on the same metrics, they will not work such as ROE in the last several years.

4. Fundamentals need time (at least 6 months) to reflect the value of the stock. You're swimming against the tide as a fundamentalist. Trading momentum stocks using basic fundamentals will not work.

5. Watch out 'Garbage in and garbage out'. Some emerging countries do not have an organization similar to SEC to ensure the integrity of the financial statements of a company and some audit firms are being paid to cover their eyes. Even though there are frauds in some U.S. companies and with their auditors.

6. The metrics may be derived from obsolete financial statements. Check out the date. The most updated one could be available from the company's website.

7. Some companies borrow a lot of money to dress up the metrics such as P/E and ROE. They will look good short-term but not long-term. Ensure the debt/equity has not been increased recently for this purpose. I recall one utility spin-off had incredible fundamentals except the debt load. It is so high that all these fundamentals will deteriorate in the future due to servicing its high debts.

Footnote

[1] The stocks are classified into sector and then sectors are divided into industries (same as sub sectors). For example, oil is a sector and oil exploration and oil services are industries under the oil sector. For simplicity, I intermix the terms here as many sectors do not need further sub classifications for this discussion.

[2] AMZN is not a value stock by any standard. As of 1/1/2013, its P/E (from last 12 months) is 157 and P/B is 15. Both fall far into my low-range values. Its price rises from 256 from 1/1/13 to 270 today (1/22/13). Today its P/E is ridiculously over 3,000. The investors are betting AMZN's internet sales will take over the concrete stores and its investors do not care about profit but rather for market share. Does it sound familiar in the internet era? Its price momentum is indicated positively by any chart. It may be a good stock for traders, but it is too risky for a swing trader and a long-term investor like me (yes, I wear two hats). I do not short stocks in a rising market, but this could be an exception.

Afterthoughts

- The only recommendation from a very popular investment book I read is to select stocks by the return of equity (ROE). I will save you the time and money to read that book. I read the entire book in an hour at Barnes and Noble's and it saved me some money / time, not to mention cutting down trees for that book. Basically it does not work today.
- DAL has an interesting Debt / Equity of over -1000% due to the negative equity. For a comparison, you may want to use Debt / ABS(Equity).

- Once in a while, I found the financial data was not consistent from different sources. Try to check out any discrepancy in the dates of the financial data of your sources. The financial statements from the company websites usually have the most updated data.

- Current Ratio = Current Asset / Current Liability. If it is below 1, then the company is having a tough time in meeting its current cash obligations.

- Dividend Yield is a valid metric for matured companies. I do not use it to evaluate growth companies or companies that need to plow back cash for research and development.

- If you use Finviz.com, you find three margins: profit, gross and operating. I prefer to use profit margin that is more useful for most companies. The other two may be relevant in some sectors.

http://www.investopedia.com/terms/p/profitmargin.asp
http://www.investopedia.com/terms/g/grossmargin.asp
http://www.investopedia.com/terms/o/operatingmargin.asp

Use Wikipedia for more description.

- Enron had millions in profits but negative cash flows. Earnings can be manipulated but not the cash flows.

  Insiders' selling usually does not cause any alarm unless excessively. Most insiders sell most of the stocks they have before these companies go bankrupt. Just common sense!

- Why fundamentals are important. (http://seekingalpha.com/article/1612442-its-shorting-season)

  On the same day when this article was published, RVLT was up 10% due to increasing sales in the earnings conference. However, the company is still not profitable. It shows how tough shorting is even with good arguments. That's why do not expect every purchase is profitable. However, with the educated guesses, you should beat the market in the long run.

- Due to my ignorance, limited time or my short period of holding stocks, I have not used intrinsic value that often.

  Book value is different from intrinsic value. Book value is calculated by summing up the values of all pieces of a company such as a building and all equipment.

  Intrinsic value is the real value of a company. When two companies have the same book value and market cap, the company that generates more profit than the other one usually has a higher intrinsic value. When the intrinsic value is higher than the stock price, it is underpriced in theory.

  The following link provides more info on intrinsic value.
http://en.wikipedia.org/wiki/Intrinsic_value_%28finance%29

3 Finviz's parameters

Most metrics are described in Finviz (via Help), Investopedia and/or Wikipedia and my chapters on P/E and fundamental metrics if available. We use the metrics for screening stocks and then evaluating the screened stocks.

The following are my personal comments and why I feel some metrics are more important than the others. Personally I divide the metrics into fundamentals and technical, which are more important for long-term investors and short-term investors respectively.

Compare the ratios to the companies in the same sector (industry) and also its averages from the last few years (5 preferable) from many other websites such as Fidelity.

From your browser, enter Finviz.com. Enter a symbol (I used ABEO for discussion). A chart is displayed with the prices and volumes for the last eleven months. SMAs (Single Moving Average) are displayed sometimes with other technical indicators. Intraday, Daily and Weekly options are available for day traders, short-term traders and long-term traders respectively.

Besides the chart and the metrics described next, it describes what the company does, analysts' recommendations (I prefer Fidelity's Equity Summary), insiders' trading and articles that are good for intangible and qualitative analysis. Many free websites such as Yahoo!Finance may provide a list of articles about the company.

"Financial Highlights and Statements" are materials for more in-depth analysis and they were more important decades ago when most financial ratios had not been calculated for you. It is important for investors with good knowledge in financial accounting. The current version also includes basic financial statements and cash flow for the current (TTM) and the last two years.

A section on Insider Trading is also included. Do not be alarmed when insiders dump small quantities of the stocks. Buying large quantities (e.g. insider transaction more than 5%) at prices close to the market price could be favorable news.

The following metrics are roughly based on the flow of Finviz from top to bottom and left to right. I skip those metrics that I believe are not too important. You can also place your cursor on the metric to retrieve the description from Finviz. Some metrics are left blank to indicate they are not applicable (zero, negative or not available). For example, the Debt/Equity of YRCW in 1/2019 is blank (same as null) due to its negative Equity. From Yahoo!Finance at the time of writing, it has a total debt of 888M.

- **Index**. Most of us trade stocks in the three major exchanges in the USA. Stocks listed over-the-counter are too risky for most of us. Skip the stocks in local exchanges and foreign exchanges unless you are an expert on these stocks and/or have insightful (not insider) information. I screen the stocks and then ignore the stocks that are not in the Dow, NASDAQ and Amex. Other screeners may let you select a group of exchanges.

- **Market Cap** (MC). To me, stocks below 50M are risky even though they could be very profitable. Ensure the Avg. Volume is at least 10,000 shares and / or your order is less than 1% of the average volume. Some small stocks are controlled by the owners and have small volumes. In this case you cannot sell your stock easily.

  Float = Outstanding shares – Insider shares.

  Usually Float does not matter as they are typically the same. However, it does for small companies with large insider shares. Most of these owners do not want to sell their family businesses and hence they reduce the chance of being acquired entirely or partially for good prices. In this case, you may have to hold this stock for a long time or you sell it at a very unfavorable price.

- If **Forward P/E** (a.k.a. Expected P/E) is not provided, use the P/E which is based on the trailing last 12 months (TTM). Alternatively, calculate the E by using the E from P/E and multiplying it by its growth rate. It may not be seasonally adjusted. I prefer using Forward P/E as it provides a better predictability power to me.

  Finviz.com leaves the P/E blank (same as null) if the earnings are negative. In this case, I would check out Yahoo!Finance's EV /

EBITDA, which also considers taxes, cash and interests. The blank condition is similar to some metrics such as when the asset is negative (they seldom occur).

Earnings Yield is equal to E/P. I call it True Earnings Yield for EBITDA / EV. It is easier to understand. Compare Earnings Yield or True Yield to the annual dividend yield of a 10-year Treasury – with the low interest rate in 2021, skip the comparison.

E/P is easier in screening and sorting the screened stocks. If you use P/E instead of E/P, you need to screen or sort stocks with a clause "P/E > 0".

When the P/E is less than 5, be careful and there may be a reason why it is so low. Many bankrupting companies have low P/Es at one time.

Compare the P/E or Forward P/E with the average P/E for the sector and its average P/E for the last 5 years that are available from Fidelity.com. Some sectors have high P/Es. If the sector is cyclical, the earnings could be affected.

When the prospect of the company is good such as Tesla in 2020, ignore P/E.

- **Cash / share**. It is used to calculate Pow P/E and Pow EY when EV/EBITDA for the stock is not available. To illustrate, if the stock is $10 and it has $10 cash / share without debt (i.e. Debt/Equity = 0), most likely it is underpriced as you can get the whole company for nothing. You should find out why the price is so low. It could be the market ignoring the stock, or there is a serious event happening such as a major lawsuit.

- **Dividend %** is useful for income investors. The payout ratio should not be more than 30% except for matured companies. Most developing companies plough back the profits into research and development, and hence they do not pay dividends.

- **Recs**. Select stocks with 1 or 2. Do not base your stock selection on this recommendation alone. There have been many bad recommendations that could cost you a fortune in losses. Use Fidelity's Equity Summary Score instead.

- **PEG** is a measure of the growth of P/E and hence a growth metric. It is similar to P/E, but it takes the expected earnings growth rate into account. The lower value is better as long as earnings are positive. If earnings are negative, then the reverse is true. It is a defect in using P/E and PEG and that's why I recommend EY (Earnings Yield) and EYG, earnings yield growth.

  If there are two companies with the same P/E, the one with a better PEG ratio is better. If two companies have the same E/P, the company with higher Earnings Growth (EPS Q/Q) would be better for similar logic.

- **P/B**. Book value (= Total Assets – Total Liabilities) may not include intangible assets such as patents. Do not trust it 100%, so is ROE which is based on the book value. Negative equity is possible when Total Liabilities is more than Total Assets. This popular metric is outdated for most matured companies as it is now made up of more intangible assets including patents, management, the quality of their employees, brand names, market share, partners, free cash flow and customer base.

- **P/S**. If two companies are unprofitable, this ratio can be used. A retail company such as Walmart is very different from a research company. This metric is only meaningful for stocks within the same sector or specific sectors.

- **P/FCF**. I prefer it to be greater than 0 and less than 50 for value investors. Most metrics can be manipulated easily, but not this one.

- **Sales Q/Q** reduces the seasonal deviation. To illustrate, retail sales for the Christmas season should be compared to the same season in the prior year.

- **EPS Q/Q**. Same as above. I prefer the growth of EPS over Sales. Both of these Q/Q ratios are growth metrics. When a company terminates its unprofitable product(s), its Sales Q/Q could be down but its EPS Q/Q could be up. In 2000, many internet companies had great Sales Q/Qs but negative EPS Q/Qs.

Q/Q comparison (quarter to quarter) takes out the seasonal variations as Sales Q/Q. I prefer both Sales Q/Q and EPS Q/Q increase. When EPS Q/Q increases far higher than Sales Q/Q, it could mean the EPS Q/Q could be temporary such as the oil company when the oil price rockets.

When the company buys its own shares, EPS could be misleading as E is fixed and the number of shares is reduced. In most cases, the fundamentals of the company have not changed.

- Positive **Insider** Transactions are favorable. Sometimes, they are misleading. Need to scroll to the end of the screen and check out more info there. If the transactions are outdated such as 3 months or so ago, and or they are purchases in a similar amount than the sales a while ago, they are not important. Insiders know the company better than us. So is Institutional Transactions as institutional investors move the market.

- Insider Own, Shares Outstanding and Shares **Float** determine the number of shares that are available for trading. A small Float with a high Insider Own limits trading and the stock should be avoided in most cases. Compare your trade position for the stock to the Avg. Volume.

- **Profit Margin**. I prefer it over Gross Margin and Oper. Margin which does not include interest expenses and taxes. When you sell software, the Gross Margin is high as it does not include development, support and marketing, etc. A retail store has low Gross Margin. It all depends on the industry, and hence it is better to compare companies in the same industry.

- **Short Float**. I prefer it to be less than 10%. If it is greater than 10%, the shorters could find something wrong with the company. If it is over 25% (indicating a possible short squeeze), I would check the fundamentals. If they are good, I would buy expecting a short squeeze potential. It is risky but it has been proven to be profitable for me.

- Technical metrics: SMA-20, SMA-50 and SMA-200. Finviz expresses them in convenient percentages. If they are all positive, it means the trend is up. SMA-20 and SMA-50 are a short-term trend and SMA-200 is a long-term trend. If you are a short-term swing investor, stick with the short-term trend and vice versa. The first two are also used as momentum grades. Many long-term investors do not buy stocks when the SMA-200% is negative.

- **RSI(14)**. If it is greater than 65%, it is overbought. If it is under 30%, it is under-bought for me. Some use 5% up or down than mine. Use it as a reference. Most stocks making new heights are always overbought, and many of these stocks keep on rising. I recommend using trailing stops to protect your profit.
- **Beta**. A volatile stock fluctuates a lot. It is good for short-term traders. A beta of 1 means the stock would fluctuate with the market, and be volatile if it is higher than 1. For volatile stocks (higher than 1), the stops should be higher. For example, if your stops are normally 15%, you may want to use 20% or even higher.
- Management performance is measured by **ROE.** It is also judged by **Analysts' Rec.** and Institutional Ownership (except for small companies). The confidence of their own ability, the company and its sector is measured by Insider Ownership and Insider Purchases.

  ROE = Net Income / Average Shareholder's Equity
  According to Investopedia, a normal ROE for utilities should be 10% while high tech companies should be 15%. Compare this ratio and many other ratios with its peers that are available from Fidelity.
- Avoid all companies that are going to bankrupt at all costs. Debt/Equity, P/FCF, Cash/Sh., P/B, Profit Margin, Forward P/E, Short Float, RSI(14), SMA20% and SMA50 would give us hints. Need to summarize all the info and study many other factors such as obsoleting products (including drugs).
- Unless you have concrete information, do not buy stocks a week or so before the Earnings Date. It is seldom to make great profits when the announcement is better than the expected.

More useful information:

- The price chart. It has a lot of features such as the resistance line. Some charts include technical indicators such as double top (a bearish warning) and double bottom (a bullish sign).

- Description under the symbol. It briefly describes what the company (sector and industry) does and its country of registration. You want to buy a stock within a sector that is trending up. For example, according to Finviz Apple is in the Consumer Goods sector and the Electronic Equipment industry.

  If you do not want to buy foreign stocks, skip it if it is not listed in the US exchange.
- Articles on the company for qualitative analysis.
- Insider trading. Pay more attention to the insider purchases at market prices. Use common sense.
- The last line lets you open Yahoo!Finance and other sites.

Other important sites

Yahoo!Finance.

From Statistics, you can find Enterprise Value / EBITDA. I call it True Yield when I flip them to EBITDA / Enterprise Value.

In case it is not available, I use Earnings Yield. In my spreadsheet without considering the cell designations,

=IF (Earnings Yield = “”, True Yield, Earnings Yield)

Fidelity

Compare the P/E of the average PE of the last 5 years. In my spreadsheet for demonstration,

Cheaper By Historically =IF(PE="","",(Avg. of 5-year PE -PE)/Avg. of 5-year PE)

Compare the P/E of companies in the same sector. In my spreadsheet for demonstration,

Cheaper By To the peers =IF(PE="","",(Industry PE - PE)/Industry PE)

Your broker's website

Your broker website should have plenty of tools to analyze stocks. As of Dec., 2018, Fidelity lets you use their extensive research free by opening an account with no position restriction. I describe some of their metrics that should be beneficial to your research.

- Equity Summary Score. Potentially good buy when it is 7 (8 for conservative investors) or higher. With some exceptions, you should avoid or short stocks if the score is 3 or below. The stocks ranking from 4 to 6 could be turnaround candidates if they are supported by good Q/Q Earnings and/or good news.

- The 5-year averages are good yardsticks. For example, in Dec., 2018, C's P/E is about 9 and the average is 14. Hence it is a value buy.

Other sources

If you have other sources (most require a subscription or being a customer), skip the stocks that have one of the failing grades. The exceptions are a new positive development and increased insider purchases.

Vendor	Grade	Fail
Fidelity	Equity Summary Score	< 7
IBD	Composite grade	< 50
Value Line	Proj. 3-5 yr. return. Also its composite rating	< 3%
Zacks	Rank	5
VectorVest	VST	< 0.7

You may be able to find Value Line and IBD in your library. Try out the free stock reports from your broker first. Finviz and Seeking Alpha should have articles (now fewer free articles from Seeking Alpha) on stocks and earnings conferences, which could have important information after separating from the "welcome" and garbage talks.

Yahoo!Finance has good info. "EV/EBITDA" is better than "P/E" as it considers debts and cash. Most use Earnings from last 12 months, which has poorer predictability than Forward Earnings to me.

When negative values such as Equity in Finviz.com, we need to adjust many related metrics or do not use them at all.

MarketWatch.com has many articles on the market in general and personal investing.

If the stock is close to the Earnings Date (found in Finviz.com), you should avoid trading the stock; as earnings could have a big swing for the stock price. Consult Zacks' ranking which is currently free for individual stocks.

Gurus

It is nice to know how gurus would rate the interested stocks. GuruFocus is a good source. NASDAQ is a simplified version, but it is currently free. Bring up Nasdaq.com from your browser. Select "Investing" and then "Guru Screeners". On the third selection, enter the stock symbol such as THO. Click "Go". You will find how 10 or so gurus would evaluate this stock in theory. Click "Detailed Analysis" for each guru.

Quick and dirty

Many times we need to evaluate a stock fast such as taking action due to some development. Refer to my other article "Simplest way to evaluate stocks". The following should take a few minutes. Bring up Finviz.com and enter the stock symbol.

Using SWKS on 6/10/16 to illustrate, Forward P/E is about 11 (fine between 3 and 25), Debt/Eq. is 0 (fine less than .5), ROE is 30% (fine greater than 5%) and P/PCF is 31 (fine if not negative).

Also, check out Market Cap, Avg. Volume, Dividend, Short Float (fine between 0% and 10%), Country and Industry. Judging from the above, it is a buy.

If you have more time, check out the following: Recom. (Ok if less than 2.5), P/B (fine between .5 and 4), Sales Q/Q (fine if not negative), EPS Q/Q (fine if not negative), Cash/Sh (compare it to Debt/Sh) and Profit Margin (fine >5%). Check some articles described for this stock.

5-minute stock evaluation

It takes even less time than the above "Quick and Dirty". However, I recommend you should spend more time researching stocks.

- From Finviz.com, enter the stock or ETF symbol. Look at the number of reds in metrics. If there are more than greens, most likely it is not a good stock.

- It should be fine if Fidelity's Equity Summary Score is greater than 8.

If you have more time, I recommend you to check the following:

- Check out Forward P/E (E>0 and P/E < 20), Debut / Equity (< 50%) and P/FCF (not in red color).

  If time is allowed, replace Forward P/E with True P/E (same as "EV/EBITDA"), which is available from Yahoo!Finance and other sources.

- SMA20 (or SMA50 for longer holding period). If SMA20 is > 10%, it is trending up.

- It is fine if the Insider Transaction is positive.
- Be cautious on foreign stocks and low-volume stocks.
- If most of the above are positive, it is likely a buy. As in life, nothing is 100% certain.

Links

PEG: http://en.wikipedia.org/wiki/PEG_ratio
Short %: http://www.investopedia.com/university/shortselling/shortselling1.asp#axzz2LNDvpemo
Openinsider: http://www.openinsider.com/
Finviz: http://Finviz.com/
terms: http://www.Finviz.com/help/screener.ashx
Insider Cow: http://www.insidercow.com/
Current Ratio: http://en.wikipedia.org/wiki/Current_ratio
How to find quality stocks.

---

http://seekingalpha.com/article/2381395-how-to-identify-quality-stocks-and-is-there-really-alpha-to-be-had

4 Intangibles

I give a score for each stock I evaluate. Occasionally some stocks with poor scores have great returns and vice versa. In general, the scoring system works. It has been proven statistically and repeatedly from my limited data.
I stick with high-score stocks with some exceptions.

Once in a while I change my scoring system to adept to the current market conditions. To illustrate, the market bottom phase and early recovery phase of the market cycle favor value more than momentum/growth. Here are some of my recent experiences and strategies:

- I double or even triple my stake on stocks with high scores. In the longer term, they are consistently better winners than the average with some minor exceptions. Besides the score, look at the intangibles described in this article.

- Watch out for the stocks with outrageous metrics such as P/E of 4 or less. It could be a big lawsuit pending, an expiration of some important drugs, etc. Also, be careful with scores in the top 5%. From my statistics they do worse than the average. Their problems may not show up in the current financial statements.

- The technology of a tech company cannot be ignored even though the company's P/E is high, that I set a limit of 25 instead of 20 for other stocks. The value of the company's technology and patents will not be shown in the fundamental metrics except from the insiders' purchases at market prices.

  For example, IDCC rose about 40% in 2 days. There was a rumor that Google was buying the company and/or Apple was bidding on it too for its mobile technology. Charts usually would flag this kind of event. For non-charters, use the SMA-20% from Finviz.com. They could be a little late as the charts depend on rising prices.

- There are more acquisitions during a market bottom (same as early recovery). The companies with good technologies are bargains and the larger companies especially those in the same sector understand their values better than most of us. These potentially profitable companies will not be shown by their scores explicitly. When corporations have a lot of cash or the credit is cheap, they are looking for smaller companies to acquire or invest in. The candidates are usually small, beaten up, low-priced and having valuable intangible assets such as technologies, customer base and/or market share of the industry segment. 2009-2012 was just the perfect environment and the before that was 2003. I had at least one stock in each of these periods and they appreciated a lot.

- The opposite is Netflix, Chipotle in 1/2012 and Amazon in 1/2013. They are over-priced by any measure. However, the mentioned companies are investing in the future. The shorters (not for beginners) are having a tough time in making money on them. When their P/Es are higher than 40, watch out. Some could be OK in the mentioned companies, but usually they are not. Do not follow the herd and your due diligence will verify whether they will still go up.

  Use reward/risk ratio. It is based on experiences. To illustrate, if the company has the equal chance to go up 50% and go down 25%, then it is a buy and the reverse is a sell.

- The retail investor just cannot possibly know about some events until they actually happen. For example, ATSC dropped 15% due to losing its second primary customer. Fundamentals cannot predict this kind of events. Charts can signal this event, but usually they are too late unless you watch the chart all day long.

- After a quick run up, TZOO plunged due to missing some negligible earning expectations. It seems the original climbing prices already had the perfect earnings growth built-in.

  I do not understand why a company loses 10% of its market cap when it missed by 1% of the expected earnings. It could be driven up and down by the institutional investors. Evaluate the stock before you act. Acting opposite to the institutional investors could be very profitable for the right stocks. Avoid trading before the earnings announcement dates (about 4 times a year for most stocks).

- The following are not easily found in financial statements: industry outlook, patents, good will, market share, competition, product margins, management quality, lawsuits pending, potential acquisition, pension obligations, advertising icons, etc. That is why we need to read articles on the stocks in our buy list or our purchased stocks.

- The financial data could be fraudulent or manipulated. I do not trust small companies in emerging markets. I have been burned too many times. Check the company names such as foreign names, ADR and their headquarter addresses (from the company profile in most investing sites).

  Earnings can be manipulated with many accounting tricks. A jump in earnings from last year may not be as rosy as it looks. Check the footnotes in the accounting statements. I usually skip financial statements unless I have big purchases in mind as my time in investing is limited.

- Cash flow cannot be easily manipulated. It is good information whether the company will survive or not, but to me it does not prove to be a consistent predictor in my tests, but an important red flag for companies on their way to bankruptcy. Examples abound.

- Repeated one-time, non-recurring and extraordinary charges are red flags.

- Stay away from the companies where the CEOs are over-compensated. As of 7- 2013, Activision's CEO raised his salary by more than 600%, while the stock lost its value in double digits.
- Value stocks. Need to know why they become value stocks (i.e. fewer investors want to own) even they are financially sound. For example, there are two primary reasons for the downfall of a supplier to Apple: 1. Apple is declining in sales and 2. Apple is switching suppliers to replace their product. Technology companies are continually building better mouse traps. They could turn around in a year or so with better products.

Conclusion

Buying a stock is an educated guess that its stock price will rise. Fundamentals do not always work, but they work most of the time:

1. When we buy a value stock, we're swimming against the tide. Hence, we need to wait longer (usually more than 6 months) for the market to realize its value. The exception is the Early Recovery phase (see the Market Cycle chapter) and it has faster and larger returns than most other stocks from most other stages of the market cycle.

2. Some metrics are misleading. Book value could be misleading for an established company such as IBM. The image of the cowboy in a tobacco company could be a very important asset that is not included in its financial statement.

3. The market is not always rational.

Afterthoughts

- Brand names of big companies are one of the most important intangibles. Here is a strategy to buy big companies in a down market. It has been proven that it works. However, do not just buy these companies without analysis.
  http://seekingalpha.com/article/1324041-buying-brand-names-in-a-bear-market-can-make-you-rich

- The reputation of a company takes a long time to build but a bad incidence to destroy in the case of GM such as the delay in recalling the killer switches.

#Filler: Carrie Fisher, another sad American story

Unless drug addiction is part of the culture now as evidenced from the legalization of certain drugs, we're in a permissive society! Brits pushed opium as a nation when they had nothing better to trade. Opium killed millions of Chinese and bankrupted China. When we do not learn from history, we will repeat history. It is another sad story of fame and money and then losing it all. I bet she would be happier in a normal life instead of being born in a privileged class.

5 Qualitative analysis

This is the last analysis to evaluate a stock fundamentally. Then the next is technical analysis which is used to find an entry point (also the exit point) for the stock.

Where quantitative analysis fails and why

I find that some stocks with high scores fail and some stocks with low scores succeed as indicated by my performance monitor. The scoring system still works statistically for the majority of my stocks.

- Reasons why stocks with low scores perform in addition to the described in the last discussion:

    - Over-sold. The institutional investors (fund managers and pension managers) dump them first, and then followed by the retail investors. These big boys will buy these stocks back when they reach a certain price range. RSI(14), a technical indicator described in the Technical Analysis article, is useful to detect these over-sold stocks. This metric is readily available from many sites including Finviz.

    - The falling price (P) improves all fundamental metrics that have the stock price such as P/E and P/Sales. However, the trend of the price is down.

    - The company has turned around after fixing its problems and/or the market has changed for the better.

    - The current problems have been resolved but not known to the public. It includes resolving a lawsuit, a new product, a new drug, or a new big order, etc.

    - Heavy purchases by insiders. The company's outlook is not shown in its financial statements. Sometimes the insiders hide them so they can buy more of their companies' stocks for themselves.

- Reasons why stocks with high scores plunge in addition to the described in the previous discussion:

- The company's fundamentals and its prices have reached or closed to the maximum heights. They have no way to go but down. It is particularly true when the stock's timing rating is at or close to the highest point. TTWO that I gifted to my grandchildren had been 5-baggers in the last few years before it plunged in 2018.

- It has reached its potential value (or a target price) and it is time for many investors to take profits.

- Sector (or stock) rotation, particularly by institutional investors who drive the market.

- The outlook of the company, its sector and/or the market is deteriorating.

- The stock price may be manipulated. There are many reasons to pump and dump the stock. Shorting is not recommended for most investors. However, some experienced shorters make money consistently when they find valid reasons to short stocks.

- It could be due to a new serious lawsuit, a new competing product or drug, canceling a major order, etc.

- Downgrade by analysts. They could spot some bad events such as product defects, violations of regulations or accounting errors / frauds. The downgrades are more important than the upgrades that could have conflict of interest.

- The financial statement had been manipulated. The SEC may ask for an investigation.

- Does not meet the consensus in earnings announcements, which have been over-acted by many investors.

Qualitative Analysis

We need to do further analysis after the quantitative analysis and the intangible analysis. Check out the company's prospects. Check out the date of the article and any potential hidden agenda items from the author. Older articles may not have much value.

Be careful on 'pump-and-dump' manipulation written by authors with a hidden agenda. It has happened especially on small companies before even SeekingAlpha.com has its share. Here was an article that tells you to sell NHTC. There was another article to tell you to buy ARTX. They fit into this category.

The sources are:

1. Seeking Alpha.
   Type the symbol of the company to read as many articles on the company as you have time for. Today this site and many other similar sites require you to be a paid member. If you cannot find too many good articles, check out the articles from Finviz.com.

   Recently, I read an article on AMD and it said it may have good profits in the next two years with the game consoles. The outlook of a company is not shown by any fundamental metric which are far from favorable.

   Following a well-known writer, I bought IBM without doing my due diligence (my fault). It went down more than 15% quickly. You can learn from my mistakes.

2. Research reports from your broker. If you do not find many, open an account with one that provides such reports. Some subscription services such as Value Line provide such reports.

3. Yahoo!Finance board. Most comments are garbage. However, once in a while you find some great insights. Usually you cannot find any info from other sources on tiny companies.

4. The most recent company's financial statements. They are usually available in the company's web site.

5. 10-Ks from Edgar database (www.sec.gov/edgar). Check out new products and its potential competition, key customers, order backlog, research and development and pending lawsuits.

6. Check out the outlook of the sector the company is in and the company itself.

7. Check out its competitors.

8. Some companies are run by stupid people. I received information via my email saying that my mutual fund account could be treated as an abandoned property. I have been cashing dividend checks every year and why it would be considered as an abandoned property. I called them right away to close my account.

   The tall and handsome guy presented articulately how he would turn around JC Penny on TV. I could tell you right away that all his tricks had been tried by other companies such as Sears, and most did not work. The intelligent investor does not care about how handsome, how articulated, how rich his family is and how many advanced degrees from prestigious colleges he possesses. If he does not make sense, do not buy his preaching and his company's stock. [Update. As of 5/2020, J.C. Penny filed for bankruptcy protection. If you had this stock and my book, you would have saved a lot of money minus $10 for my book!]

9. Check out its business model. Some business models do not make business sense and some do. Here are some samples.

- Giving razors makes sense, as the customers have to buy the blades eventually and keep on buying blades for life.

- Supermarket M lowers prices on common merchandises such as Coke and it works. They make money by providing inferior (but profitable to them) products that you cannot compare prices easily such as meat and seafood.

  Eventually there will be a supermarket in my area to satisfy me both in price and quality or at least make a good tradeoff.

- Last week it had been brutally hot. I went to a Barns & Noble's bookstore to enjoy reading the updated books and enjoyed the air conditioning. When there are more free loaders like me than customers, this business model does not work.

6 Fidelity stock research

You have to be their customer to access all their research. If you are not one already, open an account with the minimal requirements (none as of this writing) and optionally buy a no-commission ETF from them. Their research is extensive and it could be the biggest bargain. Their StarMine (Analyst Opinions or Equity Summary Score) has been proven to be a good predictor to me. Your broker other than Fidelity may provide similar tools. The following describes some of the features.

- Analyst Opinion (now Equity Summary Score or just Score). It is one of the major metrics I use in my proprietary scoring systems. They do not track a lot of small stocks. From my limited database in 7/2015 and for short durations, the results are:

Short Term: (7% return for the average)

Metric	Parm. 1	No. of Stocks	%		Parm. 2	No.	%	Predicta-bility
Fidelity Analyst	Buy	150	10%		Sell	279	3%	Good

Long Term: (8% return for the average)

Metric	Parm. 1	No. of Stocks	%		Parm. 2	No.	%	Predicta-bility
Fidelity Analyst	Buy	90	17%		Sell	208	4%	Good

- ETP (ETF to me) evaluation.
- Key Statistics. Select the industry leader by comparing the metrics to its peers. They also compare their own metrics to the average of several years. The 5-year average of P/E is useful.
- Charts for technical analysis.
- ESG Score for those who are social conscious.

Research Reports and Financial Statements give us more information about the company. It has a very good screening feature. As stated before, eliminate the number of screened stocks to a handful for further evaluation. Start with Analyst's Opinion greater than 9 and then Strong Buy in Zacks. Blue Chip Growth website is no longer free. It is easy to use Fidelity to replace their grades.

Section IV: Technical Analysis (TA)

The basics

Technical analysis (a.k.a. charting) is easier to learn than expected. It represents the trend of the market (a stock or a group of stocks) graphically. If more investors are in the market (a stock or a group of stocks), the trend is up until it changes. We divide the trends into short-term, intermediate-term and long-term.

The chartists usually do not consider fundamentals as they believe they have already been priced in the stock price and some fundamentals are not available. To illustrate, a new drug has been discovered, the stock price of the company jumps. Its fundamental metrics do not show right away but many are buying to boost up the stock price.

The volume is a confirmation. When the stock moves up or down by 10% with a low volume, the trend is not confirmed.

The trend of the stock price is not straight line in most cases. Hence a trend line is usually drawn to indicate the direction of the stock. Many believe the stocks fluctuate in certain range (or channels) and the chart draws the upper value (the resistance line) and the lower value (the support line).

When the price passes the channel, it is called a breakout. Darvas, one of the oldest and successful chartists, profited from the breakouts of the resistance line and believed the stock is close to the support line of the new channel. Hence it has a long way for profit.

If it is so simple, there will be no poor folks

It works most of the time, but do not bet all your money on it. For chartists, 51% is great (it is too for playing Black Jack). Some trends reverse very fast such as the bio drug stocks in 2015. You need to hedge your bets such as placing stop orders. Most do not want to spend their lives in watching the trend from a big screen. Most novices use too many indicators and lose to the professionals.

Simple Moving Average

The basic technical indicator is SMA. It is the average of the last N trade sessions. When N is 20 (or SMA-20), we classify it as short-term. Similarly, SMA-50 is intermediate-term and SMA-200 is long-term. This trend duration is important: You do not want to place long-term bets using SMA-50 uptrend for example. There are many modifications that I do not find them better such as giving more weights to recent data. Finviz.com includes this information without charting.

Defining the trend periods is arbitrary. I use SMA-350 to detect market plunges and SMA-100 for stocks.

Trend is your best friend

Most use TA for trending for short durations. Value investors can also use TA to time the entry and exit points for better potential profits. Value investors usually are patient and they do bottom fishing. They treat ‘oversold’ as value. TA does have indicators for detecting the bottom of the stock such as RSI(14) described next.

When the market is overbought, the technical indicator would indicate the market is peaking. Many indicators do not indicate market bottom and market peak as it depends on the market data. If the volume is low (compared to its average), the indicator may be too weak to be considered.

Many sites provide charting free of charge such as Yahoo!Finance. Finviz.com provides a lot of technical indicators without charting such as SMA% and RSI(14). It also provides screen searching for stocks that meet your technical analysis criteria.

Beginners make a common mistake by using too many technical indicators. Start with SMA (Single Moving Average). The parameter for SMA is “days”, which are actually trade sessions.

TA patterns

There are many TA patterns such as Bollinger Bands and MACD. The patterns are based on the stock prices indicate the trend of the stock. Many times history repeats itself.

Sites for TA

There are many free sites for charts with explanation of the technical indicators. Popular ones include BigCharts.com, SmallCharts.com and Yahoo!Finance. Fidelity includes some unique features such as P/E. Technical analysis depends on charts and its practitioners are called chartists, technical analysts or technicians.

Why I do not use TA for as a primary tool for stock picking

My investing style is different from a day trader. I prefer to 'Buy Low and Sell High' instead of 'Buy High and Sell Higher'. I try to find the real bottom price. TA will not find the bottom easily but it racks the trend better. As a bargain hunter, I do not expect the stock will rise fast as I'm swimming against the tide.

For some strange reason beyond my reasoning, a lot of times I placed buy orders on stocks that appreciate very fast. This is not good for me as my buy orders are usually not market orders, so I miss many big gainers.

I have many stocks losing 25% in one day. TA will not help me to sell these stocks, but stop orders might. However, a bad pattern would identify most of the coming falls.

My opinion

I do not want to argue whether TA is good for you or not. You need to find it out. Most likely, the day traders and short-term swingers will profit more from TA than the investors seeking for value for long-term gain.

Most should benefit to study the fundamentals of a stock and then use TA to enter and exit on the trade.

My current situation does not allow me to use TA extensively due to evaluating and maintaining a large number of stocks in a limited time. Most likely I am the exception. However, I do have a TA parameter in my scoring system that helps me to determine the trade decision. My investment subscription services and my personal metrics in my momentum strategy use TA more than my evaluation for bargain stocks.

Random remarks

Even if you do not use technical analysis, you should spend some time in learning it. It is better to marry fundamentals and TA. My random remarks are:

- The Institution investors (insurance companies, pension funds, mutual funds, etc.) use TA and they MOVE the market. A lot of times it becomes a self-fulfilling prophecy. It is better to join them as most of us cannot beat them.

- Day traders take advantage of the institution investors by spotting their trends.

- Most TA stocks should be good sizes and have large average daily volumes. I prefer to use TA on sound fundamental stocks.

- I do know some folks making big money using TA, but I know more making good money using fundamentals. If you marry the two disciplines, you should be a better investor. Since TA predicts the market better in shorter term, its practitioners may have to pay higher taxes (in today's tax laws) in taxable accounts.

- Our objective should be making money at the least risk. Once you claim to belong to a certain group of either Fundamental or TA, you will be biased and forget your primary objective in investing.

- The price movement usually tells the hidden reasons why it moves and its volume confirms it.

  There are many factors not shown in the financial statement such as serious lawsuits pending, market trend, insiders' purchases (based on legal or illegal information), a new product, a clinical outcome of a drug, competition, etc., but TA spots them all.

- It tracks the last two big market plunges (2000 and 2007) pretty well. The chart will not warn you right away for the upcoming plunge (as it depends on past data) to avoid the initial losses, but they will warn you to avoid bigger losses.

I use it to track the market more than on specific stocks (you can use it for both purposes).

Afterthoughts

- Steps in buying a stock. Screen stocks, perform quantitative analysis, perform qualitative analysis and lastly perform technical analysis.

  Today it is possible to do the technical analysis first to screen stocks as many web sites provide technical parameters in screening such as Finviz.com.

- Besides searching for stocks that have potential breakouts according to specific patterns, we should check the stocks we owned for potential breakdowns.

  Technical Analysis tutorial.
  https://www.youtube.com/watch?v=GENBVwV8PMs

  SMA tutorial.
  https://www.youtube.com/watch?v=Na-ctpPsnks

Links
Fidelity video: Technical Analysis
https://www.fidelity.com/learning-center/technical-analysis/chart-types-video

1 Do

When the stock, the sector that the stock is in and the market both are above its SMA-n averages (Single Moving Average for n days), it is a buy. If the volume is low (compared to its average), the indicator may be too weak to be considered.

1. Bring up finviz.com from your browser.

2. Enter SPY. Write down the SMA-200 (Single Moving Average for 200 days). Positive numbers indicate the trend for the market is good.

   However, the market could be peaking or overbought. Do not buy stocks when SMA-200 is over 5% and / or RSI(14) is over 65%. RSI is a metric in the same screen.

3. Enter the sector the stock is in. Write down the SMA-50. Positive numbers indicate trend for the sector is good.

   However, the sector could be peaking or overbought. Do not buy stocks when SMA-200 is over 10% and / or RSI(14) is over 65%. RSI is a metric in the same screen.

4. Enter the stock symbol. If your average holding period of the stocks is 50, use SMA-50 and so on. I recommend SMA-200 for holding stocks long term. Write down the SMA-n for your stock. Positive numbers indicate the trend is good.

   However, the market could be peaking or overbought. Do not buy stocks when SMA-200 is over 25% and / or RSI(14) is over 70%. RSI is a metric in the same screen.

If the above three criteria and the fundamental criteria are satisfied, most likely it is a good buy.

The next chapter on more detail on technical analysis is for future reference.

2 Technical analysis (TA)

The basics

Technical analysis (a.k.a. charting) is easier to learn than you might expect. It represents the trend of the market (a stock or a group of stocks) graphically. If more investors are in the market, the market would move upwards until it changes direction. We divide the trends into short-term, intermediate-term and long-term.

The chartists usually do not consider fundamentals as they believe they have already been priced into the stock price and some fundamentals are not available to the public. To illustrate, a new drug has been discovered, the stock price of the company jumps initially by insiders purchases and the informed. Its fundamental metrics do not demonstrate this right away, but many investors are buying to boost up the stock price as evidenced by the technical indicators such as SMA for 20 or 50 days.

The volume is a confirmation. When the stock moves up or down by 10% with a low volume, the trend is not yet confirmed.

The trend of the stock price is not a straight line in most cases. Hence a trend line is usually drawn to indicate the direction of the stock. Many investors believe the stocks fluctuate in certain ranges (i.e. channels) and the chart draws the upper value (the resistance line) and the lower value (the support line). In theory, the price of a stock fluctuates within the resistance line (ceiling for understanding) and support (floor). When it reaches its support, it becomes a buy and vice versa for a sell. Most charts including Finviz.com would display these lines.

When the price passes out of the channel, it is called a breakout. Darvas, one of the oldest and most successful chartists, profited from the breakouts of the resistance line and believed the stock was close to the support line of the new channel. Hence it would be a long way up in theory.

If it were so simple, there will be no poor folks

It works most of the time, but do not place all your money on it. For chartists, 51% is great (the same for playing Black Jack). Some trends reverse very fast such as the bio drug stocks in 2015. You need to hedge your bets such as placing stop orders. Most do not want to spend their lives in watching the trend from a big screen.

Most novices use too many technical indicators and lose in their performances to the professionals. Recently, most chartists were not doing all that great and I did not find many books on their success than a decade ago. It could be due to too many followers in similar setups. I verified it with my recent testing using Finviz.com.

Simple Moving Average

The basic technical indicator is SMA-N. It is the average of the last N trade sessions. When N is 20 (or SMA-20), we classify it as short-term. Similarly, SMA-50 is an intermediate-term and SMA-200 is long-term. I prefer 50, 100 and 250. This trend duration is important. For example, do not want to place long-term purchases using the short-term SMA-50. There are many modifications to SMA such as giving more weight to recent data, but I have not found them any better. Finviz.com includes this information without charting (SMA-20, SMA-50 and SMA-100 in percentages).

Defining the trend periods is rather arbitrary. I use SMA-350 to detect the market plunges and SMA-100 for stocks. Weighted Moving Average weighs more weight on recent price data.

The trend is your best friend

Most traders use TA for trending in a short duration. Investors can also use TA to time the entry and exit points for better potential profits. Value investors usually are patient and they do bottom fishing and they search for 'oversold' condition using RSI(14). Again high volume is a confirmation.

Many sites provide charting free of charge such as Yahoo!Finance. Finviz.com provides a lot of technical indicators without charting such as SMA% and RSI(14). It also provides screen searching for stocks that meet your technical analysis criteria.

Hands on

Bring up Finviz.com and enter any stock symbol such as AAPL. You can see the daily prices of AAPL from about nine months ago to today. Three SMAs (Simple Moving Average) are displayed as SMA-20, SMA-50 and SMA-200. The first two are for short-term trends.

When the price is above the SMA, it is expected to be trending up. Again, the trade volume is used as a confirmation.

You can also see the resistance line and the support line drawn. In theory, the stock will trade within these lines. When it exceeds its resistance line, it is called a breakout, and vice versa for a breakdown. Sometimes it displays some technical patterns such as Cup and Shoulder and Double Down (both are positive patterns).

Select Weekly data. The Candle chart is better described than the Daily chart. Candles give us better descriptions of the price: open, close, high and low. The green color indicates the price is up for the period (a week in this example) and the red color indicates a down period.

In addition, Finviz.com includes some technical indicators in the metric section such as RSI. Most other chart sites are similar in the basics. Use Finviz's Help and select Technical Analysis for more description. Investopedia has enhanced descriptions on this topic.

TA patterns

There are many TA patterns such as Bollinger Bands and MACD. The patterns are based on the stock prices and many times they prove to be correct predictions especially on stocks with high volume and high market caps. Patterns have been repeating themselves many times as they are driven by investors.

Sites for TA

There are many free sites for charts with explanations of their technical indicators. Popular ones include BigCharts.com, SmallCharts.com and Yahoo!Finance. Fidelity includes some unique features in its charts such as P/E.

Why I do not use TA as a primary tool for stock picking

My investing style is different from a day trader's. I prefer to 'Buy Low and Sell High' instead of 'Buy High and Sell Higher'. I try to find the real bottom price. TA will not find the bottom very easily but it tracks the trend better. As a bargain hunter, I do not expect the stock will rise fast as I'm usually swimming against the tide. However, value stocks could stay in the low price for a long time (i.e. value trap). I like to select stocks that turn around as evidenced by the SMA-20 and SMA-50.

With that said, my momentum portfolio has appreciated consistently and usually has the best performing stocks among all my portfolios. It is based on the timely grade from my subscriptions plus the metrics on timing.

Most chartists would also tell you to buy the stocks that have broken out (i.e. higher than the resistance line) and/or stocks at their highs. Contrary to value investing, you should exit when the trend reverses. The reversal could happen very fast and hence protect your portfolio by setting up stop loss (preferably with trailing stop) orders.

My opinion

I do not want to argue whether TA is good for you or not. You need to find that out. Most likely, the day traders and very short-term traders will profit more from TA than the investors seeking value stocks for the long-term gains.

Random remarks

Even if you do not use technical analysis, you should spend some time in learning it. It is better to marry fundamentals and TA. My random remarks are:

- The Institutional investors (insurance companies, pension funds, mutual funds, etc.) use TA and they MOVE the market. A lot of times it becomes a self-fulfilling prophecy. It is better to join them as most of us cannot beat them.

- Day traders take advantage of the institutional investors by spotting their trends.

- Most TA stocks should be good sized and have large average daily volumes. I prefer to use TA on value stocks to prevent long-term losses.

- I do know some folks making big money using TA, but I know more making good money using fundamentals. Since TA predicts the market better in the shorter term, its practitioners may have to pay higher taxes (in today's tax laws) in taxable accounts.

- Our objective should be making money with the least risk. Once you claim to belong to a certain group of either Fundamental or TA, you will be biased and forget your primary objective in investing.

- TA tracks the last two big market plunges (2000 and 2007) pretty well. The chart will not warn you right away for the upcoming plunge (as it depends on past data) to avoid the initial losses, but they will warn you to avoid bigger losses.

Afterthoughts

- Besides searching for stocks that have potential breakouts, we should check the stocks we owned for potential breakdowns.
  Technical Analysis tutorial.
  https://www.YouTube.com/watch?v=GENBVwV8PMs

  SMA tutorial.
  https://www.YouTube.com/watch?v=Na-ctpPsnks

Links

Fidelity video: Technical Analysis
https://www.fidelity.com/learning-center/technical-analysis/chart-types-video

Section V: Trading stocks

1 Order prices

Market orders

It is simply trading the stock at the prevailing market price. Place market orders only when it is necessary as stocks price can easily be manipulated especially on stocks with low trading volumes. To avoid manipulations, do not place market orders after hours.

However, in a rising market, many fast rising stocks can only be bought via market orders. Many winners never take a breather on their way up. In this case, you can only buy the stock via market orders.

Consider bid and ask. A 'bid' is the price a potential buyer would like to buy while the 'ask' is a potential seller would like to sell. Your market price is usually the worst price in either case, but it is a guarantee that you would trade the stock. A large spread would mean that it would take a longer time to use a limit order and/or the trade volume of the stock is small.

In my momentum portfolio on 11/2013, I placed a sell price for GERN far higher than the market price. Surprisingly I sold it for this price making an annualized return of 1,176% for holding it for 21 days. When there are few or no other sellers for the stock, the market price would be the price you set. If I cannot sell it in the next 9 days (30 days is my holding period for momentum stocks), I would set it lower. Update: One year later, GERN lost 29%.

Sensible discounts

I prefer to buy the stock at the price closest to the last trade price (to most it is the market price) via a limit order. I seldom lose buying these orders. Sometimes I use the day's lowest price to buy (or the highest to sell) plus a penny (or minus a penny for sell prices to sell).

My other purchase strategy is using 0.15% or 0.25% less than the current prices for stocks I really want. For some promising stocks, I buy them at almost the market price and then place another order on the same stock at 0.5% less than the last traded price (and sometimes 2% depending on the current market trend).

We all want to buy less and sell at higher prices. However, if the trade price is too far away from the current market price (such as 5% from the market price), these trades may never be executed. I have had a long list of buy orders that were not executed and turned out to be big gainers. Learn from my bad experiences.

Use a good discount (such as 10% from the market price) if you believe the market, the sector or the stock will dip by 10%. After you bought the stock, you place a sell order 10% more than the price you paid for it hoping the stock will return to the original price and you pocket 10%. Wishful thinking! However, it has happened to me several times primarily due to temporary market dips.

It works when there is a correction and/or the stock is very volatile. It is usually within the 5% range to take advantage of these situations, not the 10% as described. For a 10% plunge, it usually is due to some serious problem of the company surfacing. One common reason is not meeting its earnings expectation and in this case it usually continues its downward trend.

Larger discounts on a falling market

During a falling market (or a mild correction), 3% less than the current prices for buy orders may be fine for some stocks (use 5% for volatile stocks). To illustrate, I placed about 10 of these orders over the last two months during a market dip. Most of the orders were filled. When the market is plunging, do not buy any stock.

Caterpillar and Cisco were some of my buys at these discounts. They were in my watch list to buy. Initially these shares often fall even lower as the trend was downward. As of 12/18/12, CAT earned me from 3% and 14% (bought in 6/12 and 7/12) and CSCO bought in 7/14/12 returned about 34%. My original objective: Buy deeply-valued stocks, wait and sell them when the economy returns.

When you predict the market will dip by 5%, set your buy orders accordingly. Again, predictions are just educated guesses. From my experience, they work most of the time but not all of the time.

On the day of the earnings announcement, the fluctuation of the stock is usually high. Check any change in the earnings estimate before the announcement and act accordingly. Zacks is supposed to be a useful tool to predict earnings estimates. Do not leave orders during the earnings announcement dates, which can be found in Finviz. When the earning turns out to be good, the stock price surges and your order will not be executed. When the earnings are bad, the stock price will plunge usually and you most likely over-payed.

Option expiration dates usually cause more volatility. Retail investors do not have to be concerned except you may use wider stops. In theory, dividend days have little effect on the stock price as it will be lowered by the dividend amount.

High volume of a stock could mean opportunity

High volume usually increases the stock price volatility. If the volatility of a stock increases substantially (such as doubling its average daily volume), there could be important news on the company, recommendation changes from a major analyst or trading by the institutional investors. It usually takes the institutional investors a week to trade a stock with their sizable positions.

Many times it is started by the insiders who know about the breaking news of a stock before it is publicized. Some investment services / sites specialize in identifying the increasing volumes on these stocks.

Because day traders do not want to leave any open positions overnight, higher volatility occurs at the end of the day. It is the same on the day (usually on Friday) when the options are expiring.

Monitor your trade prices

You cannot tell whether you are paying a fair price without keeping a record. To illustrate, you're paying 1% less than the market prices in buying stocks. You may have missed buying some winners. If the 1% you saved is smaller than the appreciation of the stocks you would have bought at market prices, then you should adjust the buy prices to 0.5% less than the market price and monitor again.

Market trend makes a difference too. When the market is trending up, buying any stock would most likely be profitable and usually the purchase orders with higher discounts will not be executed.

Follow the same logic on sell orders. Need to have at least 25 stock purchases (and potential purchases) to make the conclusion meaningful. If you do not trade a lot, you will not have enough data to verify. As described, I prefer not to place an order during the earnings announcement dates which can be found in Finviz.com. If you cannot buy the stock, consider to use market order the next day. With most brokers offer no commission trades, the "All or none" option is not valid.

Good prospects

When you find gems especially those stocks that are followed by analysts, buy them at market prices and consider doubling the bet if you are really sure you have a winner. From my super stock screens, I spotted NHTC. I placed several bets and one market order. All of them were NOT executed except with the market order. At the end of the day NHTC is up 18% and my executed order is up 14%. I did not have the best buy but made a good profit. NHTC was on its way to a huge appreciation and I sold it too early. I have earned not to sell a winner and protect the profit with a stop.

Lower the buy for risky stocks (if the beta from Finviz is greater than 1 for example) even if they have good fundamentals.

Quality over quantity

If your time is limited, spend all the time on researching one stock one at a time. However, you need to own at least 3 stocks (more stocks for a large portfolio) for your diversification purposes.

Double your normal purchase position on stocks that look great after the research. For risky stocks that look good, you may want to halve your normal purchase position to cut down on the risk. If you are less risk tolerant, do not buy risky stocks at all. My results are not conclusive on risky stocks but I do get a good sleep.

A recent example

Recently I sold EA with $1 more than my order price but $2 less than the current price of the day, which was the earnings announcement day. I do recommend not placing orders right before the earnings announcement day for the stock. If the earnings are good, you do not get all the profit as in this real example; my broker did get me $1 more. If the earnings are bad, you will not sell it any way. It is the same for buying stocks.

Afterthoughts

- Besides luck, the smart investor never sells at the peak but usually within 10% of the peak. No one can predict the peaks consistently.

- I made mistakes like most of you. One time my buy price was higher than the last price executed. Luckily my broker adjusted it to the right price but I may not be that lucky next time. Several times I switched the buy price and sell price by mistake. One time it was due to my boss coming by that forced me to enter my order hastily.
- Some experts do not suggest their clients to buy stocks on the way down. With respect, I offer opposing arguments.

    - It is fine to buy them on the way down, if you have the conviction that the company or the economy will recover.
    - No one knows where the bottom is, but averaging down could be beneficial if the company or the economy can recover. Check why its stock price is falling and whether the company can fix its problems. Some major problems are only temporary or easy to fix.
    - Most of my big profits are made by buying close to the bottom prices on stocks that have a good potential to recover.
    - Many value stocks are on sale when the market dips. The most favorable time is in the Early Recovery, a phase in the market cycle defined by me.
    - Most experts agree that: The best time to buy is when there is blood in the street. It is demonstrated by the year 2003 and 2009.
    - Contrarians never follow the herd, but you need to have a good reason to be contrary. I recommended Apple in 2013 when every institutional investor was dumping Apple.
    - Stocks are manipulated via selling shorts. When the shares of a stock to short (like over 30% of shorts) are running out, there is a good chance for a short squeeze. Ensure the company being shorted heavily is not heading into bankruptcy.
- Make good money when you are right only 45% of the time by: 1. Limit your losses via stops and 2. Place higher stakes on stocks with higher appreciation potential.

- Some make money on earnings announcement (found in Finviz.com). Earnings would amplify the stock price by at least 5%. Once in a while, there are exceptions. In the last quarter of 2015, Disney posted great results, but the stock dropped. It could be that the market even expected better results or the market is not rational. I believe the later in this case.

Links

Selling short:
http://en.wikipedia.org/wiki/Short_%28finance%29
Short squeeze:
http://en.wikipedia.org/wiki/Short_squeeze
Fidelity Video: Stop Loss.
https://www.fidelity.com/learning-center/trading/trailing-stops-video

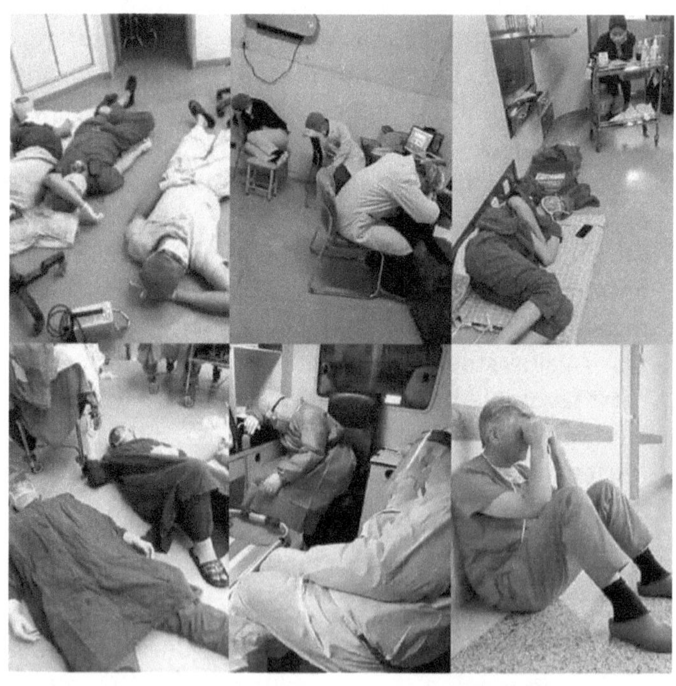

They are more important than ALL entertainers and athletes.
Not taken by me but copied from the web.

2 Stop loss & flash crash

You can limit your stock loss with stops. There are some incidents where you do not always want to use a stop loss.

- Flash crash (May 6, 2010 also August 2015).
  It would turn your stops into market orders that could be substantially lower than your stop prices. Some brokers offer stop limits, but they do not guarantee the orders will be executed.

  The better way is a "mental stop" (my term). You do not place a stop order but place a market order to sell when your stock falls below a pre-defined price. During flash crashes, you do not want to place the market orders to sell but place orders to buy from your watch list.

  I bought some stocks at more than 10% discount during the flash crash (actually I could buy them even at better discounts) and within a week most had returned to the prices as before the flash crash.

  Placing buy orders with huge discounts to the market prices works better for volatile stocks. You should cancel the unexecuted trades before the weekends / holidays and reenter them afterwards to avoid unexpected events that may affect the stock prices.

  Avoid trading drug and bio tech companies with huge differences to the market prices. High tech is a good sector for this purpose and fluctuating 10% in this sector is more of a norm than an exception. Buying an ETF at 5% discount is a better bet than buying specific stocks from my experience.

- My experience with 911.
  I sold many stocks due to stop orders during 911. The market came back in the next three days and I missed the recovery from the stocks that were sold and did not buy back them in time.

- If your stocks are rising, you need to adjust the stop loss prices accordingly. To illustrate- in maintaining a 10% stop loss, your stop is at 90 when the current price is 100. When the stock price rises to 200, it should be adjusted to $180 (10% less than the current price). It is also called a trailing stop. Need to review these rising stocks, and change the stop price periodically (one week to one month depending on how volatile is the stock)).

Most brokers allow you to enter most trades "Good till Cancelled". Even for that there is an expiration date such as 6 months for Fidelity. Fidelity's trades for Short Sell expire by the end of the trade session. Check your broker's current policy.

- Risky markets.
  When the market is risky, you may want to use a stop loss. To prevent another flash crash, you may want to use a 'mental' market order. It is not perfect, as it requires constant watching of the market.

  There are many investing services and sites that give you the 'right' prices for a stop loss. Basically it depends on how volatile are the specific stocks. The chartists will tell you under normal conditions stocks are trading between the resistance line and the support line. Use the stop loss just below the resistance line to avoid the stop order from being executed due to the volatility of the stock.

  For simplicity as I have too many stocks in my portfolio, I use a percent. In the old days, it was recommended 8% or so below the prices you paid. In today's volatile market, I recommend 12%.

- Risky stocks.
  A stop loss is the only way that you can limit your loss for big drop (such as 25%). Affimax lost 85% of its stock value in one day with the news that three of its patients died.

- Low-volume stocks.
  The market order could drive the prices right down as there are few buyers in low-volume stocks. If there is only one buyer, he will buy with the best price for him (or the worst price to the seller).

Unless I have good reasons, I would skip the low-volume stocks. I define low-volume: If my buy amount is higher than 1% of the average daily amount (= average daily volume * stock price).

- Beta.
  Stocks may be more volatile than the market. Beta is used to measure its volatility. The market can be measured by the S&P500 index. If the beta of a stock is 1, its volatility is the same as the market. If it is 1.2, it is 20% more volatile.

  Set a lower stop loss for volatile stocks to prevent stocks from selling due to regular fluctuations. If your regular stop is 10% below your buy price and the beta is 1.1 (10% more volatile), use 11% rather than 10%.

Afterthoughts

Let me show you my bitter experience. The following are 5 stocks I wanted to buy and the average return was quite good.

Stocks	Return
URI	63%
GMCR	572%
MTW	186%
PII	-74%
TSCO	-127%
Avg.	124%

I placed buy orders at 5% less than the market prices as most 'bargain' investors do. I bought both of the two losers but no winners. The winners never took a breather on its way up, but the losers went down. I did buy GMCR via a market order in my momentum strategy in a separate account.

3 Short selling

You sell short a stock because you believe it is going down in price. It could be used to hedge the downside of a related stock you own. Shorting should be avoided for beginner investors.

Advantages

You believe the stock and or the market (using contra ETFs that represent the market) is going down.

What to buy & how

If Fidelity's Equity Summary Score for the stock is below 4, it is a short candidate.

The following are my suggestions on shorting stocks that have the potential to go down. Basically these stocks are both fundamentally unsound and technically unsound. Many sites (some require paid subscriptions) provide a composite grade for fundamentals and technical. Finviz.com does provide most of these metrics and many are used in the following discussion. If you combine the following metrics, then most likely you may need to compromise on some metrics to make your decision to short or not.

- Fundamentals

    - The price is more than four times the book value.
    - EY is negative. Negative PEG is another consideration.
    - High debts (Debt/Equity > .5) except for industries that require high debts.
    - Insiders are unloading their company's stocks. They do this for many reasons. But, when they are buying, do not short the stock as they may know some positive events we do not know.
    - Bad intangibles such as losing market share and/or a major lawsuit(s) is pending.
    - Read articles on the company from Finviz, Fidelity, Seeking Alpha, etc.

  - Do not short stocks that are on their uptrend. It includes the current marijuana stocks that most have no fundamental values and/or historical data.
  - Do not short small stocks with a small market cap or float. I usually short stocks with a market cap or float > 200M. Use higher values for conservative investors.

    The stocks with small floats may be controlled by the owners – if they do not sell, the stocks available to trade will be limited. Another indicator is the Avg. Daily Vol.

- Technical metrics:

  - Do not short when the stock plunged more than 10% recently. It could mean the bottom has been reached.
  - Overbought (RSI(14) > 60). There may be a reason, so it is only a secondary consideration. Most stocks to be shorted may have RSI(14) < 30.
  - The momentum metrics such as SMA-20 and SMA-50 are important too. SMA-20% from Finviz.com should be negative.
  - Some sites especially the paid sites may give you a momentum grade. Select the stocks with a bad momentum grade (a.k.a. timing grade) but not the worst grade (as it has nowhere to go but up).

- Trading considerations
  - Do not trade in the first hour (first half hour for me) as there may have new developments overnight.
  - Your short trade (limited order) may only be valid for the day; check this with your broker. It is good for your trade too. For example, I placed a short sell order for MRSN and it was cancelled at the end of the day. The next day it was up by 16%.
  - Your broker may need to approve whether you can short stocks.
  - When you sell short and are using limit orders, enter a sell price higher than the last trade price just like selling a stock.
  - Close the short position when your trade loses a pre-defined percentage which depends on your personal tolerance.

Disadvantages and some suggestions

- Short stocks when the market is plunging and limit your shorting positions when the market is rising.

- Could lose more than 100% of the investment.
  Actually, in theory, there is no limit. If the shorted stock price rises by 10 times, the loss is well over 10 times the money invested. The 2015 example was Weight Watchers. The price boosted up by more than 170% when Oprah took out a position on them. Fundamentally this stock was not sound and it should be shorted. No stock pickers can predict that. Use mental stops to protect your trade.

- Need to pay dividends and interest for the shorted stock.
  The higher the dividend rate for the stock, the more you have to pay. Experienced investors should avoid high-dividend stocks when shorting unless the expected shorting period is only brief.

  In addition, you need to pay interest for 'borrowing' the stocks to sell. Brokers charge interest rates differently and it could be huge savings to shop around if you short stocks a lot.

- Need both fundamental and technical analyses.
  From my experience, technical analysis is more important than fundamentals in shorting.

- If shorting a stock is successful and closed within a year, the gain is usually subjected to the short-term capital gains taxes which are typically higher than the long-term capital gains taxes. Check current tax laws.

- Not all of the stocks can be shorted. Your broker may not have the stock you want to short. It is also possible that your broker can close out your short positions for various reasons. Check the margin status with your broker.

- Selling short is not allowed in retirement accounts as of 2016. However, you can buy contra ETFs for a group of stocks to bet against the market or a specific sector, but not on a specific stock in retirement accounts.

- The following sectors are riskier: the drug, mine, bank (unless you know the quality of their mortgages) and insurance sectors. An approval of a drug could drive the stock price up by more than 25% in one day. The same for earnings announcements. It could drive the stock more than 25% in either direction.

- Your screens may find many stocks in bio tech companies. These companies especially with a market cap of less than 1B have the worst fundamentals. However, when they have a new discovery, the stock prices could rocket. Do not short them when insiders are buying (Insider Transaction in Finviz.com) and high SMA-20% (from Finviz.com).

- There is no perfect timing. Some stocks fluctuate a lot with no rational reasons, or the prices are driven by institutional investors. Some stocks could be manipulated. The shorted stocks could move up for a long time until they finally crash.

- A bad company could be acquired by another company due to a good buy; it could boost its stock price.

- Use mental stops (i.e. set a price you can afford to lose and when it reaches the specific price, place a market trade to exit the shorted shares. You do not want to make 5% several times and lose 50% in one trade.

- You may not want to short companies that are fundamentally unsound with a good momentum. They may have good prospects such as improved profit, being turned around, settling a lawsuit and/ or new products are being legalized and/or approved. If you do, then use mental stops to protect your trades.

- Watch out for short squeezes when the short percentage approaches over 25%. In a nut shell, the stock is running out of shares to be shorted. As a result, it would rise in price especially on any good news. As of 8/2015, I expect short squeeze for PPC and SAFM (CALM in 12/2015) for the following reasons:

  1 The shorting has no bases. It is most likely from one or two hedge funds.
  2 Fundamentally sound.

3 Beef will be replaced by a lot of healthier and cheaper chicken if not already, esp. during the drought in California.
4 In Hong Kong for example, they do not allow live chickens imported from China during the bird flu breakout, but they did allow frozen chicken from the USA if there was no political game going on.

Put Option
It is similar to shorting a company with more advantages than disadvantages. It is not for beginners.

Margin

Margin should not be used extensively. It is expensive and most brokers try every trick they can to squeeze profits from all transactions to subsidize their low-commission incomes. Usually you can borrow up to 40% of your current position and the rules and the margin rates vary among brokers.

Many investors had losses during the last two market plunges. However, many including myself had made a killing in 2003 and 2009 using margin. I use it for the following reasons.

- For convenience in placing buy orders that exceed my cash position in my taxable accounts.

- I can pay back my outstanding margin loans from my home equity loan (check the current tax laws) as it is far, far lower than my broker's margin interest rates. However, I do not recommend this for conservative investors.

Links & Articles
Tilson
Put Options.http://en.wikipedia.org/wiki/Put_option
Fidelity Video: Options.https://www.fidelity.com/learning-center/options/finding-options-strategies/options-analysis-tool-video
Fidelity Video: Selling short.https://www.fidelity.com/learning-center/trading/selling-short-video

4 Covered calls

For basic descriptions on a covered call from Wikipedia, click here or enter (http://en.wikipedia.org/wiki/Covered_call) in your browser.

It is like collecting rent from the apartment you bought. The difference is that the renter has an option to buy the apartment at a preset time and price.

The rent is quite substantial if you do good planning. To start with, you want to buy stocks that have a market to sell. Usually they are large companies with high trading volumes.

Since one contract is for 100 shares of a stock, you cannot sell a covered call on 50 shares of a stock. On the other hand, when you have 1,000 stocks, the commission of 10 contracts would be more than the cost of 1 contract depending on your broker's schedule.

It is time consuming to keep track of the covered calls but it is well worth your time and effort. If the stock price exceeds the strike price of your covered call, you may want to buy the same shares back, so you would not miss any further appreciation of this stock.

However, if it is in a taxable account and you have a loss in a forced sell, do not buy it back otherwise the tax loss is not allowed (i.e. a wash sale) for the year as of 2016. When the contract expires, you may want to start another contract on the same stock if the stock has not been sold.

Covered calls do have their disadvantages such as higher commission rates and sometimes forcing you to sell at a higher tax rate for short-term capital gains in taxable accounts. It is avoidable by using covered calls on stocks that are qualified for long-term capital gains. In addition, you need to buy them back when they increase in price beyond your strike price or lose its potential to appreciate further. Using another put could keep you from not losing any gains beyond the strike price. However, I prefer to use my time in more productive ways and this insurance is not cheap. One's opinion.

One company advertises their techniques using covered calls which could give their users 3 to 6% monthly returns. If you believe in this fantasy, you do not need this book. There is no free lunch.

My recent experience

I sold Netflix covered calls with the strike price about 2% higher and a 3% premium (from my memory) but the price shot up 12% higher in one day, so I was potentially losing 7% profit. However, it turned out to be a good experience as Netflix went downhill later (8/2012).

Normally I prefer to sell covered options for stocks with a quantity from 100 to 600 shares (i.e. 1 to 6 contracts) for the longest time (about 2-3 months). Some non-volatile and small stocks are not candidates to write covered calls on. Some stocks are not optionable. Typically high-tech stocks have a higher premium to be collected as their stock prices fluctuate more. The right stocks can generate 10% or even more a year in addition to the fluctuations of the stock prices.

In general, if I feel the market will be down for the period, I use covered calls especially for stocks holding over one year (unless I have short-term loss to offset any short-term gains) in taxable accounts. Watch out for any tax change that may affect your total return.

Recently I attended a sales pitch on a 3-day training course on a strategy for making 24% per year and it is quite possible especially with the S&P 500 returns about the same. I wish it were available to me 15 years ago. It seems to be too good to be true.

How to sell covered calls

First you need to open an account with your broker and apply to trade options including covered calls.

Check how your broker charges commissions. Ask how much they charge for one contract and 10 contracts of a stock.

The covered call is an agreement to sell the rights to the buyer of the stock at the strike price for a specific date range (a.k.a. expiration date). Typically options expire on Fridays.

You need to write covered calls on the stocks you already own. One contract is 100 shares of stocks. Check out the option chain to select the price, expiration period and the strike price. Normally, the strike price should be higher than the current market price. You may want to have an expiration date 2 weeks or longer. When the contract is expiring in a few days, the contract has little value and most likely the small 'rent' is not worth the risk and the commission.

When the covered call is sold, you receive the 'rent' immediately and any dividend during the 'rental' period.

When the option is 'called' due to a price rise above the strike price, your stock will be sold and you will have to pay the regular commission.

At this point, evaluate the stock to check whether you want to buy it back. If the stock surges, you may have to pay a higher price – thus losing the extra appreciation. In addition, you may have to pay a higher capital gains tax if it is held less than the required period for long-term capital gains in a taxable account.

Note. Notice that some stocks are not optionable and/or not practical to write options on. Most brokers charge a flat rate for the first contract (such as $7) and an incremental fee for each additional contract. Shop around as the fees vary if you write a lot of covered calls.

The best stocks for covered calls are large US companies with a large average volume. The option (a.k.a. the 'rent') pays better for volatile companies such as high-tech companies. From my rough estimates for illustration purposes, the annualized return on covered calls for AAPL is 25% and C is 12% after commission.

5 Diversification

LTCM, a hedge fund run by smart people, and Isaac Newton both made one serious mistake about investing. They both bet all in one bet and they lost it big. They were the smartest folks on earth but they violated one basic principle about investing: diversification.

Another example is the potato. Irish made good living in their primary crop: potato. When a virus came, they lost all the potatoes and caused the potato famine.

Diversification improves a portfolio's performance in the long run and it reduces risk. Diversification includes other asset class besides stocks such as oil, gold, cash (yes even cash as a safety net to grasp better opportunities ahead), real estate, etc. However, stocks historically produce the best return. In addition, most stocks are quite liquid as it takes a minute to sell them compared to selling a house for example. You can buy other assets such as gold (GLD), money market funds and real estate (via REITs) via the low-cost ETFs.

When an asset is over-valued, it will return to the average historical value with one or two exceptions. Gold is one exception, but it is partly due to the depreciation of USD and the previous prolonged downfall of gold adjusted to inflation.

Simply put, owning 10 to 15 good stocks with less than three stocks in the same sector (which have to be good sectors to start with) achieves diversification goal for most. When one sector crashes, you still have two more good sectors.

Every one's situation is different:

- Depends on your wealth and your age.
  For younger folks with limited wealth (less than $50,000 to invest), a portfolio of 3 stocks (preferably most in ETFs) in different sectors or one diversified ETF could be enough. Your objective about investing is saving money for a down payment for a house, paying your loans including college loans and/or improving your earning power by taking classes.

  Retirees may want to maintain a larger percentage of your holdings in cash and/or invested in bonds (long-term bonds could be very risky when the interest rates is going up). Those wealthy enough can fully invest in stocks as losing 50% of their portfolio doesn't alter their lifestyle. Most business owners should invest in stocks and other vehicles instead of plowing back to their businesses in order to diversify their investments.

Portfolios with more than a billion dollars such as in most mutual funds owning 10 stocks with 100 million each are just too risky to me.

Holding cash is safe but it loses its value due to inflation. To illustrate this point, consider these three scenarios in 1950:

1. An apartment bought in for $10,000 in NYC or in your home town.

2. An investment in the Dow Jones 30 Industrials for $10,000.

3. A 3.5% certificate of deposit or one of the U.S. Treasuries for your $10,000.

By now, all real estate investments should have appreciated many, many times over and most stock shares value would have multiplied also. The $10,000 CD gain has lost real value due to inflation. Our capitalist system punishes us for not taking risk. In the long term, risk is smoothed out over time.

- Excessive frequency in re-balancing your portfolio for diversification takes up time from evaluating stocks. It may cost you in transaction fees but they are low in today's self-directed brokerage accounts. In addition, it may have some tax consequences in taxable accounts.

The advantage of churning the portfolio (but not excessively) can improve the quality of your portfolio with most updated information about the companies you invest in.

Many brokers display your current diversification in your monthly statement summaries. If not, use a simple spreadsheet to classify the sectors and the asset classes in your portfolio.

- Diversification can easily be achieved by buying indexed funds and/or ETFs. They are less volatile. I recommend it to all folks with less than $50,000 to invest.
- Diversification does not mean to pick simply a stock in other sectors that has the opposite correlation from the stocks you own. The stock quality comes first.
- Diversification takes a back seat to spotting market plunges. When most stocks plunge such as during 2007-2008, diversification does not save your portfolio, but spotting and reacting to market plunges will.
- Some of our stocks will lose value. If they were due to our mistakes, write them down and learn from them. If they were frauds (not avoidable in many cases), diversification would limit our losses
- Over diversified is not too good either. With too many stocks you own, you may not have time to monitor them. Focus investing could be very profitable.

My suggestions on diversification

Portfolio up to	**Strategy**	**For stock pickers**
$ 50,000	ETF that simulates the market	5 stocks
$100,000	80% in ETF and 20% in a sector ETF(s)	10 stocks
$500,000	10 stocks with less than 3 in same sector.	15 stocks with less than 3 in same sector.
$1 Million	15 stocks + at least 20% in ETFs.	20 or more stocks depending on your time available and less than 4 in same sector.

As described, everyone's situation is different. If you have more time for investing, you should be able to handle more than 10 stocks. Playing market timing (i.e. switching to cash) depends on one's risk tolerance. If you are good at stock picking, you should buy stocks instead of ETFs. On a personal note, I usually have more than 10 stocks.

6 *When to sell a stock*

There are many reasons to sell a stock as follows.

Personal

1. Has met the targets/objectives.
   It could be 10% gain in a very short-term swing, x% return in 4 months for a short-term swing or y% gain after a year for long-term trades. Define x and y depending on your risk tolerance and how often you trade.

   I bought 4 stocks in one day during the August, 2015 correction and placed sell orders with 10% more than my purchase prices. I sold one in a day and another one within a month.

   Never look back and do not blame yourself when the prices are better than your trade prices. When the market is volatile, use a higher percent of the current prices. Be disciplined. Stay on the same strategy and detach yourself from emotions.

2. Realize that we have made a mistake. Do not let our ego blocking our eyes. It could be due to bad analysis, unexpected frauds, lawsuits, and/or bad data. It is better to get out with a small loss. I prefer 25% loss as a threshold. A trader may prefer 10% or even less.

   We have to ensure whether it is a mistake or not. If the 'mistake' is just bad luck or due to conditions we cannot possibly predict or control, then it is not a mistake. If it is a mistake, learn from it. When we diversify, one bad loss would not cause a big dent to our portfolios. Stop loss is a good tool most of the time except on flash crashes.

   If the criteria have been faithfully followed and it does not work well, check out whether your criteria are wrong or it does not work on the current market conditions.

3. When we have too many stocks in the same sector, we want to replace some stocks to diversify our portfolios.

When the sector is rising, we want to weigh more on the sector at the expense of diversification, and vice versa. Set a limit of how many sectors you are holding.

4. Need cash for living expenses.

5. To reduce tax burden by selling some losers. Tax consideration should not be the primary reason for selling. Take advantage of the favorable tax treatments of long-term capital gains. In short, sell losers within the short term and sell winners after 365 days; check current tax laws.

   Harvest tax losses. Sell losers and buy back similar stocks. It is not too clear that you can buy back the same loser in your children's account under the current tax law. Avoid wash sales that you cannot incur the tax loss for the same year.

6. To take advantage of low tax. In 2013, we can pay virtually zero (except the increase of tax on social security payment) Federal income tax on long-term capital gains when our income is below a specific tax bracket (15% as of 2015). Check the current tax laws. Evaluate the sold winners for possible buy back.

Market Timing

7. When the market or the sector plunges, sell stocks.

   For temporary peaks, do not sell all stocks, but those stocks whose fundamentals have been deteriorated more than the other stocks in your portfolio. The objective is to raise cash for buying opportunity.

Deteriorating appreciation potential

8. There may be some stocks that have better appreciation potential than the ones you currently own. Churning the portfolio by replacing better stocks may cost some brokerage commissions and taxes, but it improves the quality and appreciation potential for the entire portfolio.

9. The company's fundamentals have changed for the worse. If you use a scoring system, compare the current score with the score you bought the stock. Apple is a good example from 2013 to

2015. Buy when the fundamentals are good and sell when they are not.

The common ones are expected P/E, the earnings growth rate and the sales growth rate.

When they have passed the peak and started to decline, sell them. When they are heading to bankruptcy, sell them fast.

Hints that the fundamentals are degrading

Evaluate the stocks you own at least every 6 months and check their daily news at least once a week (easily done using Seeking Alpha's portfolio function).

- The cash flow is decreasing fast. Cash flow is not a particularly good predicative indicator for appreciation, but a good indicator on whether the company will survive. This metric is very hard to be manipulated.

- A new or pending lawsuit. Check how serious is the lawsuit and minor lawsuits can be ignored.

- When the SEC pays attention to a company, it usually means bad news.

- Increasing receivable and/or inventory.

- Big drop in sales. Do not be alarmed when a new product or a new drug is going to replace a major product. Compare sales to the same quarter of prior year to avoid seasonal fluctuations (easily done using Finviz.com).

- Short percentage is increasing fast – someone found something wrong with the company.

- The invalidity of 'one-time charges'.

- Abnormal return rate of the company's pension fund comparing to the average of the companies in the same sector.

- The extravagant life style of the CEO and the many easy loans to officers.

- Too many and too costly reconstructing charges.

- Earnings have been restated too many times.

- Deceptive accounting practices have been discovered.

- A successful product from the competitor or the current product is losing its market share or becoming a low-profit commodity.

- Insiders and/or institutional investors are dumping the companies' stocks far more than the averages especially in heavy volumes and by more than one insider.

    - Have more than one insider dumping a lot of the stock within a month and no insider purchase in that month.

    - Have more than one insider decrease their holdings by more than 10%.

- The entire stock market is plunging as indicated by our chart in detecting market crash.
- The stock price does not move up with good news. It shows the price has peaked.
- The accumulation amount is far less than the sold amount. When the stock price is up, the accumulation is less than the sold stocks when the stock price was down last time. It indicates no more accumulation ahead and hence the stock will be down most likely.
- Management deteriorates. One hint is the deteriorating ROE from the last quarter.
- Poor operations. They include recalls of products such as the GM recall on ignition switches, product secrets being stolen and customers' credit card info being stolen.

Selling a winner

Even with the above, you may still hesitate to sell a winning horse. It is human nature. Set a stop loss (say 10% below the current price) mentally. You want to do it mentally as you want to avoid flash crashes or events you do not have control of such as 911. You do not want to sell your stocks in such events. Adjust the stop loss price when the stock price rises. You will benefit for rising stocks by not existing prematurely. In another words, let the winners rise.

You define the conditions of a previous peak by using SMA-200% or SMA-50% (from Finviz.com), RSI(14) and P/E. Sell the stock(s) when these conditions happen.

Alternatively, sell the stock when it is in or past the upper Bollinger band if you feel the stock will not have a breakout (i.e. price crosses above the resistance level).

You may have two rights for every wrong prediction of the price direction. Most investors should take profits. It is easier to make 50% on a stock and find another stock to gain 35% than making 100% in the same stock. Of course, there are exceptions.

Remember that the fall of a stock is usually faster and steeper than the rise. Do not fall in love with any stock.

Afterthoughts

- Another article on this topic.
  http://buzz.money.cnn.com/2013/04/05/stocks-sell/
  An article from Investopedia. Nothing new but it is worth to have the same second opinion.
  http://www.investopedia.com/financial-edge/0412/5-tips-on-when-to-sell-your-stock.aspx

It also depends on your strategies. I sell most of my stocks in my momentum portfolio within a month. At least one strategy I know does not keep any stocks during the peak stage of the market cycle – the easiest time to make money but also the riskiest time.

7 Trade plan

You should have a trade plan. It should include the following basics:

1. Objective.
2. When, what stocks and how many to buy.
3. When and what stocks to sell.
4. When and how to monitor your trading strategies.

The follow is my suggestion. Adjust them according to your personal requirements.

Be disciplined

It would make your trading to be a discipline which will provide better results in the long run and save you time. Following the trade plan would not allow your emotion to take over.

To illustrate, you have a specific day (Monday or the first day of the month) to check the value of your portfolio. Checking it several times a day is a waste of energy and it could cause harm to your emotions.

Objective

Set up your objective and requirements first. Your objective could be seeking the highest profit, profit at the least risk, protecting principle, generating income or a combination. Beating the market should not be your primary objective.

For example, a better objective is making more than 5% per year in the next 10 years at the least risk. Why 5%? I estimate we have 3% inflation and 2% taxes.

You can be conservative and aggressive at the same time by setting up two accounts, one for each objective. In addition, you may want to define the maximum investment amount for each account.
I have three objectives and they usually fall into different accounts and different holding periods.

- Profit at the least risk. Buy value stocks. Review bought stocks every 6 months. Non-taxable account.

- Momentum. Buy momentum stocks for maximum short-term (1 month) profits. Roth account.
- Conservative. Define a larger safety net. Conserve cash. Move all to stocks only when the market is most favorable.

Contrary to the above, most investors' or traders' objective is beating the market by a specific percent. It is fine too to measure how you perform against the market. For ultra conservative investors, not losing money is the primary objective.

If you made 10% and the market was up by 20%, you did not do good performance wise. However, do not blame yourself if your primary objective is conserving wealth. Most likely you had a high percent of your portfolio in cash and/or safer investments which do not appreciate a lot but they conserve your wealth.

Be flexible

Every one's trade plan is different. You should start a simple one and add features that would be useful to you. Keep it simple as you will not follow a complicated one.

Other features are: how you screen stocks, your average holding period, tax consequences, performance monitor, etc. This chapter shows you the very basics of a trade plan and you should start one if you do not have one.

You can refer to any chapter of this book in your trade plan. To illustrate, refer to the chapters when to sell a stock and spotting market plunges.

You can change your objective. When the market is risky, you want to be more conservative for example.

Disciplined but adaptive

Stick with the plan consistently. When your strategy that has been proven before does not work now, you should still stick to it. It is a common mistake for traders switching different technical indicator when the current one does not work. It explains why most beginner traders lose money.

It should be adaptive. When the current market favors growth, stick with a growth strategy.

A sample trade plan

You can review what stocks to buy and sell once a week or once a month depending on how active you are in the market. List the criteria you want to buy. Define your average holding period for a specific objective. Also define when and why you want to sell a stock.

Personally I prefer to have two sections: Common Tasks and Specific Tasks. Common Tasks includes 4 categories: Weekly Tasks, Monthly Tasks, Quarterly Tasks and Yearly Tasks. Evaluate stocks to buy on Tuesday every week for example. Update the portfolio and check out the chart on marketing timing on the first week of every month. Review performance of the portfolio quarterly (or half a year). Perform year-end tasks.

Specific Tasks include tasks I have to do on specific dates such as filing tax return, transferring stocks to my children and renewing investing subscriptions.

Weekly Tasks:

Mon	Covered calls
	IBD-50 review
Tue	Momentum strategy
Wed	Sell Momentum stocks over 2 weeks.

Monthly Tasks:

Mon	Performance monitor.
	Market timing: Market & Correction.
Tue	Find stocks using selected strategies.
	Find stocks using screens.
Wed	Evaluate stocks
Thur.	Buy stocks
	Sector rotation.
Fri	Evaluate any stocks to sell.
Any	Monitor momentum performance.

Quarterly Tasks:

1	Monthly tasks.
2	Performance monitor.

Year-end Tasks:

1	Tax adjustments for taxable accounts.
2	EOY purchases.
3	Spreadsheet for taxable accounts.
4	Fully invested in Dec. 15-Jan. 15
5	Screen performance monitor.
6	Dogs of DOW.

Review your performance and the trade plan

If you do not know what you did, how can you know what you're going? Review every trade transaction and monitor their performances.

Learn from your losses. Did you stick to the trade plan? If you lose too many times and/or take too much risk (evidenced by many losses and/or big losses), you may have to modify your trade plan. However, the trade plan may not be good to the current market (for example trading growth stocks in the bottom of the market cycle).

If you have to let the winners get away too often, review what's wrong. Sometimes, a lesson is not a lesson but just bad luck.

Learn about yourself

Learn about your risk tolerance, how mentally prepared are you on big losses and big wins. If you have more money than you can use for the rest of your life, conserving wealth should be your primary objective.

To illustrate with a portfolio of one million, your average stock position is $100,000 if you only have time to follow 10 stocks.
To many, the portfolio with 10 stocks is quite risky. You may consider having 10 stocks of $50,000 each and invest the rest ($500,000) in ETFs, mutual funds and/or bonds. Ensure no three or more stocks (some prefer 2) are in the same sector.

Prepare for some losses. Reduce the average loss to small amounts. I prefer 25% maximum loss for volatile stocks and 20% for other stocks. Some prefer using stop loss orders of 10% to 15% loss. Today's market is too volatile to stop losses less than 15%. One's opinion. You should have some big winners but let them getting away by selling them too early. One way is to use stop orders (10%

less than the market price) and adjust the stops periodically (say a month) for the appreciating stocks.

A quick way

Write down your objective and what tasks you do every week, month and year in the inside back cover in this book (hard copy only). If you do not do it now, you will never do it.

Trade journal

Keep a journal of your trades and ideas. Review it from time to time why you bought a specific stock. It is far better than recalling the experiences from memory.

Everyone should have a book such as this one to record their experiences. I do not recommend publishing one. You should spend your time in investing. Unless you're famous, most likely publishing is not profitable.

It should be part of a trade plan. You use it to monitor your performance of your trade. When you use a screen that is for short term, you want to exit the trade accordingly. When the screen does not perform, it may mean the market is not favorable to this screen and you should skip using it with actual money. Here is a screen shot of mine. I group the trades under different screens.

	A	B	C	D	E	F	G	H	I	J	K	L	M	N	O	P
1	**Performance**			Prce		$					Date			Return		Status
2	Stock	QTY	Account	B.P.	S.P.	Buy $	Sell $	Profit	Curr P.	% better	Buy Date	Sell Date	Days		Ann. Ret	
3	LAKE	2,000	401K	10.93	13.99	21,860	27,975	6,115	9.45	48%	07/15/15	11/24/15	132	28%	77%	S
4	ABTL	1,500	ROTH	16.60	18.50	24,900	27,750	2,850			07/16/15	09/10/16	422	11%	10%	B
5	ELMD	5,000	401K	4.01	4.22	20,054	21,095	1,041	4.81	-12%	03/17/16	04/07/16	21	5%	90%	S

The formulae are:
B.P. (Buy Price) =IF(B3="","",IF(D3="","",D3*B3))
% better =IF(I3="","",(E3-I3)/I3)
Days =IF(K3="","",L3-K3)
Return =IF(D3="","",(E3-D3)/D3)
Ann. Ret =IF(N3="","",N3*365/M3)

Add any columns you want such as Account.

8 Tax avoidance

Tax avoidance is a good way to save some money legally. Tax laws change all the time. Check Wikipedia on current investment taxes. Consult your tax lawyer as my knowledge in taxes is limited, and the tax laws are always changing.

In general for Federal returns on your taxable accounts (as opposed to IRA, Roth IRA, IRA-Rollover and 401K), you have to pay taxes on dividends either at the ordinary income rate or at a qualified rate which is usually lower. If the stock that was held longer than a year, you pay long-term capital tax (max. 20%). The short-term capital tax rate at the ordinary income rate up to 37%. In addition, you may have to pay state and local taxes. Currently, you can offset $3,000 or up to your total losses from your regular income.

Do not implement what I did as tax laws change frequently and every one's situation is different. Here is what I did and I hope it will be applicable to you.

- Sold most profitable stocks that I held more than a year in taxable accounts in 2011 to qualify for long-term capital gains. Usually they have more favorable tax treatments than the short-term capital gains, which are treated as ordinary income. I bought some back. I maintained a 15% tax bracket, so the tax bill from Uncle Sam is virtually 0 (not exactly due to more tax on social security and Medicare as a result of the trades). I still had to pay state tax. As a retiree, I can control my income.

- Converted part of my Rollover IRA to Roth in 2012 and 2013. I paid taxes today. However, the Roth conversion gives me tax-free appreciation for the future trades in this account and it will lower taxes and my minimum withdrawal requirement in the future. Check whether it is still available.

- The taxes from dividends in the retirement accounts are deferred but eventually they will be treated as regular income when they are withdrawn. Very few people have higher income during their retirement. If you are the lucky few due to the successful investing in your retirement accounts, you may end up with a higher tax bracket during your retirement, particularly when you are forced to withdraw at age 70 ½.

- Gifted some appreciated stocks to my children. The current price of the gifted stock is used in calculating the total cost allowed, not the price you paid for them. I prefer the value stocks that have potential for long-term appreciation. It is good for them and not good for Uncle Sam. You can gift up to $15,000 (in 2019) for each spouse to each child without paying any Federal tax. For a family of four, you and your spouse can gift up to $60,000 (= 15,000 * 4) a year.

  The link: https://www.irs.gov/businesses/small-businesses-self-employed/frequently-asked-questions-on-gift-taxes

  The cost basis of the transferred stock is quite complicated. Check out the current tax law. The cost basis of the appreciated stocks are carried to the receiver, so it would lower your capital taxes as most of us are in higher tax brackets than our children.

  From my experience, the cost basis of the depreciated stocks after the transfer is the market price on the transfer day as of 2016. I do not understand it enough to comment but just to tell you what I have experienced. I tried to offset my son's unexpected short-term capital gain by transferring a losing stock and that does not work.

- My lawyer set up trusts for me including my house. They will avoid probate hopefully. From the current tax law (as of 2016), the cost basis of your stocks will be stepped up or down to the stock prices on that day you pass away. Ask your heirs to keep a business paper for the stock prices or tell your brokers to adjust the cost basis on the day you pass away. Of course, you have to tell your heirs now to take care of these tasks. Again, ask your tax lawyer for details.

  Make sure you specify the beneficiaries in your and your spouse's accounts to avoid probate. Check your local state laws. Some states take more than a year to finish the probate process for a house. As of 2014, my state (Mass.) has an exemption of 1 million, not portable to your spouse, and they calculate the entire estate when it exceeds the exemption. There is no estate tax if my estate is a million dollar. I have to pay a rate on

1,000,001 if it just exceeds it by one dollar. That's why we should move 30 miles north to New Hampshire.

I estimate that it takes about three years for the average estate to be distributed. You want to cut down the duration by having a will to start with, so you do not want to pay extra for your lawyer.

- At age 70 ½ (as of 2016), you are required to withdraw them in a schedule and it could put you in higher tax bracket. Roth withdrawal is not counted in the mandatory withdrawal for a person's lifetime as of 2016.

- Roth IRA if qualified could be the best deal for most. However, you have to use after-tax money to fund your Roth IRA.

- I simulate my next year via my tax preparation software and adjust my income accordingly.

- Most oil partnerships and many MLPs require you to file special tax forms for non-retirement accounts in 2017. I avoided most of them as my time is limited. Some ETFs require you to file the complicated K-1 (vs 1099) in your tax return. You can find this requirement in ETFdb.com. You can avoid them by not buying these ETFs; I prefer to buy them in my non-taxable accounts (i.e. retirement accounts). Usually the taxes on these dividends are lowered as they are treated the return of investment after depreciation.

- Avoid wash sales in your taxable accounts http://en.wikipedia.org/wiki/Wash_sale

  You cannot claim the loss for the year if you buy back the stock within 30 days. Before I buy, I check whether I sold this loser in the last 30 days. Before I sell a loser, I check whether I bought it in the last 30 days.

  I placed one order to sell a loser at a higher price and another one to buy it back at a lower price. When there is a big swing in price for that stock, both orders were executed within 30 days. I cannot claim the loss of the sold stock for that year. However, the loss can be adjusted to the cost basis of the newly-acquired stock as of 2013.

There are many ways to avoid it. Try not to buy it back within 30 days (check the current regulation) and this is the best way. IRS has more restrictions and it is better not to push it to the limit. Buy a similar stock in the same sector. Buy it in your children's account. Again, check the current tax laws.

Afterthoughts

- Tax audit signs.
  http://money.cnn.com/gallery/pf/taxes/2014/03/14/tax-audit/index.html?iid=HP_LN
  Your business would be treated as a hobby if you do not have a profit in three out of the last five years. Day traders and businesses can deduct all the trading expenses. Some form an investing company in some Caribbean island to avoid paying taxes. Again check the current tax laws.

- As of 2013, the dividend tax is at 20% max. Do not believe it is no tax in tax-deferred accounts. When you withdraw, it will be treated as a regular income and it can be as high as almost 40% (as of 2013). Your dividend tax rate depends on your income.

- When you trade 5 times or more a week, investigate whether you're eligible to trade as a business by the current tax rule. A business allows its owner to deduct business expenses.

- Fidelity: Investment tax.
  https://www.fidelity.com/learning-center/mutual-funds/tax-implications-bond-funds

  ETF Taxes on Foreign Stocks:
  http://seekingalpha.com/article/2491465-foreign-withholding-taxes-in-international-equity-etfs

Links
Tax Avoidance:
http://en.wikipedia.org/wiki/Tax_avoidance
Tax Law:
http://en.wikipedia.org/wiki/Income_tax_%28U.S.%29

Section: VI Strategy

A strategy is how to find stocks (usually via screens, also known as searches), analyze the stocks, buy them and sell them. This section concentrates on screening for stocks.

I read the book What Works on Wall Street by James O'Shaughnessy blaming many other strategies for non-performance. Later I read another book mentioning that O'Shaughnessy did not work after he published his book.

As mentioned in this book, the strategy will not be effective when too many investors chasing the same strategy. That's the reason I provide you with many strategies and you should explore newer strategies yourself. The market favors different group of strategies in different stages of the market cycle. For example, when the market is at its bottom, it favors value stocks.

The best way to check what is the favorable strategy is to test the performances of your different strategies for the last three to six months. With today's PC and several low-cost subscription services available with historical database, it is a simple and feasible task.

There are many different approaches to strategies such as "Buy low and sell high". We have to match the proper strategies to the current market conditions. To illustrate, if the market is in Early Recovery, a stage in the market cycle defined by me, value stocks have better appreciation potential than growth stocks, which perform better in the Peak phase.

Traders and hedge fund managers change their strategies frequently. Retail investors should do the same.

One strategy was the poster boy for a subscription service. It worked well before. I tested it recently and it was one of the worst strategies. The lesson is: There are no evergreen strategies. Test out whether they still work in the last 90 days.

This section concludes that there are many strategies but select those strategies that work in the current market conditions.

Fidelity Video:
Trading strategies
https://www.fidelity.com/learning-center/trading/types-of-trading-strategies/overview

The following are two related books I wrote.

Finding Stocks.
http://ebtonypow.blogspot.com/2013/10/finding-stocks.html

Best Stocks in 2014 According to Me. Check out any future book on the same topic.
http://ebtonypow.blogspot.com/2013/11/reserved_5358.html

Screening stocks

It works for me with about 40 screens. I check out the recent performances periodically and select the top screens (about 10 usually).

Before looking for stocks, check out whether the market is risky. After screening, I score the screened stocks and do further evaluation before I purchase any stock.

When we follow all the above, there is no guarantee that we'll make money. In the long run, we do and it is far better to follow a discipline than without.

Here are some free sites for screens.

There are more described in this article or type the following
http://stocks.about.com/od/researchtools/a/071909screenlist.htm

1 Tom's conservative strategy

The following is a summary of Tom's conservative strategy as described in his profile in Seeking Alpha web site. Use it as an example and modify it to fit your investing philosophy. You need to ignore your friends telling you how much money he is making when the market is up. You also need not to tell them how much money you're not losing otherwise you do not have any friend.

Click here for Tom's strategy. Ignore the date posted as this is one of the very few strategies that are evergreen. As of 12/2015, it does not perform well during 2009 (or 2010) to 2015 due to the long, unexpected rising market. However, it beats the above two strategies by good margins in the long run.
(http://tonyp4idea.blogspot.com/2012/05/tom-armisteads-investment-strategy.html)

A winning strategy for couch potatoes

My friend John has a very similar strategy similar to Tom's. My friend is making money with the least risk. He only buys stocks after the market crashes and sell stocks when the market rises. Ignore all market pundits. It is recommended to anyone who does not have time to monitor his/her investment.

He bought stocks in 2008-2010 and sold them after 2010. It was very profitable for him in 2000-2008 using this simple strategy. However, he missed the gains from 2010 to 2015. It is unusual that we have such a long bull market. I beg he is still beating most mutual fund managers with this simple strategy that does not require much work.

Enhance a good strategy

Following the favorable stages to trade in the market cycle described in this book:

- Buy SPY in the Early Recovery phase (about 1 ½ year after the crash or use the entry point described in Market Timing in this book.
- Sell SPY in one or two years after the buy.

Here are some options if you have time to watch the market.

- Buy stocks (or an ETF that stimulates the market) in Nov. 1 and sell them in May 1. I prefer buy in Oct. 15 and Sell in April 15 to avoid the herd.
- Buy stocks in Dec. 1 and sell in Feb. 1 to take advantage of the best (statistically) period of the year.
- Buy stocks in the year before election and sell them after a year.
- Add long-term bonds when the interest rate is high (say more than 5%). Switch to short-term bonds or cash when interest is low (say less than 2%).
- If you have time, time the market by following my simple technique to exit and reenter the market.

Spend the rest of the time in the comfortable couch (i.e. enjoying life) or sip some fancy tropical drink served by some beautiful tropical lady in some nice tropical island. Not a bad strategy! Of course, the market is not always rational and there is always risk involved.

An alternative to Tom's strategy

Have a list of value stocks to buy and update the list periodically (say every 3 months).

When the market loses 5%, buy them at 2% less than the market prices or alternatively 5% less than the prices in your list.

Decide when to sell such as making 12% profit or losing 12%. If the market is not risky, you may want to keep them longer. It should work in a sideway market but not during market plunges.

John's Strategy

John maintains about 75% cash and only buys blue chip stocks at 52-week low. He ignores friends telling him making good money when the market is up.

Here are my changes for better returns at the expense of taking more risk. I would maintain 50% cash and 0% in Early Recovery, a phase in the market cycle defined by me. I would also include all stocks with market cap over 1 billion and stocks close to 5% of their bottoms. In addition, I would evaluate the stocks before I buy as some stocks may go to zero.

Jill's Strategy

Jill does not have time for investing. She subscribes to an investing service. She prepares a list of stocks to buy. For illustration only, the stocks should have Safety 1 or 2 in Value Line or VST grade higher than 1.25 in Vector Vest. When the price reaches the price she is willing to pay, she does another research with her subscription service and check the fundamental rating in Blue Chip Growth. If they are good, she buys it and usually keeps it until the market is risky.

Beautiful 'girls' of Thailand

Top-down investing

The nutshell is described here. Only buy stocks when the market is favorable. Find the best industry (a subsector) and then find the best stock(s) within the selected industry. In doing so, our chance of successful investing is substantially increased.

It is so simple and it has been proven by many including myself. I just wonder why it has not been extensively practiced. I offer a simple trade plan as follows:

1. Do not invest when the market is plunging. I have a simple way to detect market plunges without any expensive subscriptions or tools.

2. Select the best industry (most are represented by an ETF or ETFs specific for the industry or sector). For example, Technology is a sector. Computer and Software are industries (subsector under Technology). From time to time I use sectors for simplicity and most free sites do not sub divide the sectors into industries. Check out the best-performed industry or sector from last month in many sites including SeekingAlpha and CNNfn.

   If you're a value investor, you may not want to choose the timeliest sector but the most under-valued sector. Value investors should hold the sectors/stocks longer (such as 6 months or even longer) for the market to recognize their values.

   In addition, you need to detect the sector/stock rotation by the institution investors who control over 75% of all trades (i.e. smart money). They will rotate sector/stock when they find better profit potential in another sector/stock. Use stops to prevent further losses.

   If you do not have time to research on stocks, trade ETFs for sectors and skip the next step.

3. The final step is to select the best stock(s) within the sector via fundamental analysis (including intangible analysis), insider trading analysis, institution trading analysis and technical analysis.

   Do not let these terms scare you. We will start with the simplest approach without any subscription and a lot of effort.

4. The next step is when to reevaluate and sell the stocks when conditions change or they meet your objectives. If the market is plunging, sell all stocks.

Stick and repeat the entire process.

The easiest retirement planning system

Have a budget and live within your means. Buy good stuffs that last for a long time. After saving enough cash for emergency and planned expenses such as vacation, new car, college, etc., invest your extra money in a retirement account (Roth IRA if allowable) with 80% in a market ETF and 20% in a short-term bond ETF.

Run the chart described in the market cycle chapters once a month. If the chart tells you to exit the market, move all to cash. Reenter the market when the chart tells you so. It beats most if not all of your financial plans from the best experts money can buy.

Afterthoughts

My late friend had a 'buy and hold strategy' that worked pretty well. Most of his stocks were big companies. He died with a house worth more than a million and many millions in stocks. His only mistake was not to transfer more of his stocks to his heirs before his death. He died on the year when the estate exemption returned back to a million. Uncle Sam was the biggest winner and won big without any effort.

2 Dividend investing

This is a popular strategy now. It is expected to be so for the next 10 years or until the average CD rate beats the average dividend rate. We have a lot of retirees who depend on incomes from investments. The low interest rates in CDs and bonds drive these folks to dividend stocks.

Here is a simple screen to find these stocks. First find the stocks that have dividend rate more than 2% (about half of the S&P 500 stocks). Take out those sectors that give dividends as a return of equity (REITs and many partnerships). Eliminate the stocks with bad fundamentals such as high expected P/E, high debt (compared to companies in the same sector), etc. Next ensure they should have a good history of maintaining or increasing dividends (i.e. dividend growth).

As of 5-2014, it has been working for the last five years if you also follow my article to be cautious on bank stocks, the drug companies, the miners, the insurers and small foreign companies. In addition the stocks with good dividends fluctuate less in prices especially during market plunges.

However, when a strategy is over-used, it may not work anymore. There may be a mild bubble on these dividend stocks (due to too many followers). We will discuss how to protect our dividend portfolio.

In addition, we should not buy (actually should sell most stocks you own) stocks during a market plunge. I will describe how to detect market plunges and corrections. Since 2000, we have two market plunges with an average loss of over 45%. We hope to have a maximum loss of 25% and are ready to return to the market as indicated by the simple marketing technique described in this book. There are at least three variations on dividends:

1. Dividends given to stock owners (registered on and before the ex-div date).
2. Covered Calls. You can receive dividends while ‘renting’ your stocks.
3. DRIPs, Dividend Reinvest Plan. http://en.wikipedia.org/wiki/Dividend_reinvestment_plan

The basics

Basic ratios for dividend stocks

- Ex-dividend date

You will be eligible for dividends if you have your stock on the record. You want to buy the stock earlier or on ex-dividend date in order to receive the dividend.

- Payout Ratio

It is the dividend / profit. Too high a ratio may not be good as the company does not plow back the profit into research / development. Most mature companies has higher payout ratio as they do not need to plow back into research / development comparing to high tech companies.

The other option of using the company's cash is stock buyback that would increase the stock value in theory.

Earnings per share = Earnings / Outstanding Shares.

When 'Earnings' is fixed but Outstanding Shares are reduced, the ratio looks good deceptively.

- Dividend Yield.

It is dividend / price.

Why companies pay dividends

Companies can use the profit by plowing back into research / development, buying back its stocks, acquiring companies and/or giving dividends to the stock holders. In theory, the company should consider the option most beneficial to the average stock holder. In practice, the management tries to benefit them by choosing the option best to appreciate their stocks and hence their granted stock options.

My additions to conventional dividend investing

Hopefully my additions would improve the performance of this strategy that has already been proven to work.

- I add market timing to Dividend Investing. You need to sell most stocks before a market plunge and buy them back as indicated by the chart.

- Diversify your portfolio. Keep 10 stocks for a portfolio less than a million. Ensure not more than 3 stocks in the same sector. Keep 20 stocks for portfolio over a million. Too many stocks would require more of your time that would be better spent in evaluating individual stocks. Too few stocks would impact your portfolio when one stock has a big loss.

  It is just a recommendation. Vary your holding size and holding period according to your time, your portfolio size and your expertise in investing.

- Stick with stocks over $2, average daily volume over 10,000 shares (8,000 for stock prices over $25) and market cap over 200 million.

  Most big winners usually are in the price range between $2 and $15 price and market cap between 200 million and 800 million. They represent the stocks that big boys are ignoring due to their restrictions. This is just a general guideline. Change them according to your requirements.

  I prefer to skip stocks from most emerging countries, especially the smaller companies as I do not trust their financial statements.

- Ignore the subscription services or books claiming making over 30% consistently. Some even have examples of making 5,000%. Most likely they tell you the winners but not their losers.

  Check whether their portfolio uses cash or not as it cannot be cheated. I bet those portfolios consistently making over 30% are not real. Alternatively they have 10 portfolios and they only show you the one that makes good profit.

  When they back test their strategies, they cheat their performances with survivor bias (i.e. those bankrupt stocks are not in the historical database). If their returns are that great, do you think they will share their secrets with you?

> Some made a big fortune and lost it all. So, the turtle investors who make small profits consistently and keep most of the wins fare far better than making millions in a year and losing it all the next year. Market timing and diversifying our portfolio help us win consistently in the long run.

Besides screening dividend stocks yourself, there are many sites providing this information. You can google 'dividend stocks'. The following are some of them.

TopYields
http://www.topyields.nl/Top-dividend-yields-of-Dividend-Aristocrats.php

An ETF on Dividend Aristocrats
http://etfdb.com/index/sp-high-yield-dividend-aristocrats-index/

From Wikipedia on S&P Dividend Aristocrats
http://en.wikipedia.org/wiki/S&P_500_Dividend_Aristocrats

There are many sites to screen dividend stocks. I select Finviz.com that should give us the best result and are free. In addition, we use the same site for market timing.

Screening is only the first step. Need to filter the good ones from the bad ones.

DRIP stands for dividend reinvestment plan. It uses the dividend to buy more stock of the company that pays the dividend automatically and most likely with no commission and sometimes at 2-3% discount.
I participated in these plans before. After a long while, the stocks bought from dividends worth more than the initial stocks. Need to keep track of the cost basis of the bought stocks when you sell these stocks. Check out whether the company and/or your broker offer such program. There are many sites to have more info of DRIPs such as Money Paper (https://www.directinvesting.com/).

More on dividend stocks

- Here is a site (currently free) to grade dividend stocks. http://navelliergrowth.investorplace.com/dividend-grader/

- As of 2016, dividend yield has a maximum Federal income tax rate of 23.8% compared to 43.8% from other income rate. Hence, the dividends in the retirement accounts besides Roth IRA may cost you more in tax.

- It makes sense not to choose the stocks with top 25 dividend yield stocks. If the yield is that good, they could have some problems. It also could be yesterday's darlings. Try the next 25 according to an article I read. Need to further analyze each stock especially on the fundamentals. Ensure the high dividend yields are not due to return of capitals as in some REITs and partnerships; it could be the reason why the top 25 dividend yield stocks do not perform.

- From my friend Norman:
  Use CCC charts by David Fish.
  http://dripinvesting.org/tools/tools.asp

- A good article on dividend stocks.
  (http://seekingalpha.com/article/1591272-the-7-habits-of-highly-effective-dividend-growth-investors?source=kizur)

- Check their payout ratios. When the company plows back most of its profit to dividend, the company will not grow much. Many mature companies are fine in doing so. A payout ratio between 50-70% is good to me.

- Ignore the Q4 of 2012 in identifying dividend and dividend growth stocks. It is a period when companies pay extra dividends expecting higher tax rates for their stock holders next year that does not materialize.

  REITs must pay out 90% of earnings to maintain REIT status. Their dividends are taxed as ordinary income.

- Buffett on dividends.

(http://kinderflow.blogspot.com/2013/08/dividends-warren-buffett.html)

- Buy the companies that have a lot of cash and do not pay any or much dividends. There is a good chance these companies will pay dividends or increase their dividends and the stock prices would usually appreciate. If the fundamentals do not change much, sell them afterwards.

- As of 7/2013, corporations have a lot of cash and low debt comparatively. Coupled with low interest rate and a weak economy, corporations increase dividends and buy back their own stocks.

- A successful story on dividend investing.
 http://finance.yahoo.com/news/heres-janitor-amassed-8m-fortune-234459317.html

- Here are another set of criteria for dividend stocks.

    - Dividend yield over 2.5% (or at least .5% above the average of S&P dividend yield).
    - Dividend growth for the last 5 year is zero or higher.
    - Profit growth is positive for the last 5 years.
    - Dividend payout is under 70%.
    - P/E under 25 and earning is positive.
    - ROE is over 8%.

  If you do not find too many stocks, the dividend stocks may be overbought.

- There are many other sources for income besides dividends:
    - You can sell some shares. Check out the tax consequences.
    - Buy bonds. Long-term bonds are favorable when the interest rate is high. Check S&P's bond rating. Forget the bonds BBB and below.
    - REITs and energy royalty trusts. Many require you to file extra forms if they are in taxable accounts.

3 Define Insider Trading

Investopedia defines it as:

"Insider trading can be illegal or legal depending on when the insider makes the trade: it is illegal when the material information is still nonpublic--trading while having special knowledge is unfair to other investors who don't have access to such knowledge. Illegal insider trading therefore includes tipping others when you have any sort of nonpublic information. Directors are not the only ones who have the potential to be convicted of insider trading. People such as brokers and even family members can be guilty.

Insider trading is legal once the material information has been made public, at which time the insider has no direct advantage over other investors. The SEC, however, still requires all insiders to report all their transactions. So, as insiders have an insight into the workings of their company, it may be wise for an investor to look at these reports to see how insiders are legally trading their stock."

If you need more information, click this link from Wikipedia.
http://en.wikipedia.org/wiki/Insider_trading

My additions to conventional insider trading

Hopefully my additions improve the performance of this strategy that has already been proven to work most of the time.

- I add market timing to Insider Trading. You need to sell most stocks except contra ETFs before a market plunge and buy them back as indicated by the chart.

- Diversify your portfolio. Keep 10 stocks for a portfolio less than a million. Ensure that there are not more than 3 stocks in the same sector. Keep 20 stocks for portfolio over a million. Too many stocks would require more of your time that would be better spent in evaluating individual stocks. Too few of stocks would impact your portfolio when one stock has a big loss.

It is just a recommendation. Vary your holding size and holding period according to your time, your portfolio size and your expertise in the sector.

- Stick with stocks over $2, average daily volume over 10,000 shares (8,000 for stock prices over $25) and market cap over 200 million.

  Most big winners usually are in the price range between the $2 and $15 price and market cap between 200 million to 800 million. They represent the stocks that big boys are ignoring due to their restrictions. This is just a general guideline and there are always exceptions. Change them according to your requirements.

  I prefer to skip stocks from most emerging countries, especially the smaller companies as I do not trust their financial statements.

- Ignore the subscription services or books claiming they are making over 30% consistently. Some even have examples of making 5,000%. Most likely they tell you the winners but not their losers. It is easy to pick up winners that fit their strategy but it does not tell you the real performance.

  Check whether their portfolio uses cash or not as it cannot be manipulated such as using the best prices of the day to trade. I bet that those portfolios consistently making over 30% are not real. Alternatively they have 10 portfolios and they only show you the one that makes a good profit.

  When they back test their strategies, they cheat their performances with survivor bias (i.e. those bankrupt stocks are not in the historical database). If their returns are that great, do you think they will share their secrets with you?

  Some made a big fortune and lost it all. So, the turtle investors who make small profits consistently and keep most of the wins fare far better than making millions in a year and losing it all in next year. Market timing and diversifying our portfolio would help us win consistently in the long run.

4 How to profit from insiders

My own monitor

The following is one of my performance monitors from the stocks I bought for over a period of 6 months.

All stocks	Stocks with Insiders' Purchases	Beat all stocks
21%	28%	33%

This test was performed on 9/7/2013. They were the actual stocks I screened from the screens that had been proven. Insider Purchase is one of the fundamental metrics I monitored. The total number of stocks is 372 and 77 are identified as having heavy insider purchases. The returns are not annualized (annualized returns are better to compare stocks bought on different dates) and dividends are not added. Most stocks have a holding period longer than 6 months.

The test results are consistent with my previous tests. Beating all stocks by 33% is quite convincing. It does not take a genius to show the strategy of following insiders' purchases works at least in this performance monitor.

I conducted another test using the web site OpenInsider on 11/2013. It listed all the insiders' purchases for more than a year. Selected insider purchases about 1 year ago by the Officer (CEO and CFO) only. I skipped the purchases that do not meet the requirements.

The annualized return is 50%. I only had about 50 stocks and it is not enough evidence to draw a conclusion. Even with 40% return, the strategy proves itself again.

My suggestion

Evaluate the purchased stocks again in 6 months. Sell the ones whose fundamental metrics have deteriorated or the price targets have been met.

Consider market timing. Sell most stocks when the chart indicates that the market is plunging.

Consider the total return. If you can wait for a month or so for less taxes on long-term capital gain, do so. If you expect that your stock does not appreciate a lot in the next few months, consider covered calls (similar to collecting rent with the renter's option to buy the housing unit at a specific price and time).

A recent example

Sometimes all experts are wrong on a stock except the insiders. Today (2/5/2015), GLUU is up by 23% with a good earnings report. It is 31% up since I bought it on 1/28/15, just 8 days ago. The annualized return must be astronomical.

I bought it based on the favorable Insider Purchases and confirmed by a good earnings rating (second best) from Zacks. Pow EY was 7% (passed), short-term score 4 (failed), long-term score 16 (just passed) and Pow Score 2 (just passed). The quarter-to-quarter profits and sales were spectacular at 200%.

The experts were wrong when I evaluated the stock: Safety Margin ridiculously negative, Blue Chip Growth C, Shorter 17%, Fidelity Analyst 4 (1 to 10 with 10 the best), ROE 3%, SMA %(10, 20 and 200 days) all negative (not good), IBD composite grade 33 (far below the average) and its SMD grade D.

Filler: How to fight terrorism?

It is interesting Poland has zero terrorist attacks so far and they refuse refugees. So is Japan.

Most of the countries that have most terrorist attacks are those who welcome Middle East refugees. I like to help them but we have to ensure we do not let terrorists in.

They are called terrorists or freedom fighters. We have bombed their cities so bad that they have no future. They cannot fight us back with their primitive weapons but using terrorism. Every action has a reaction.

---

5 Sector Rotation

Sector rotation has been proven to make good profits at the least risk if it is properly implemented. This book improves your odds in making profits than traditional schemes in sector rotation by:

- Market Timing. When the market is plunging, do not buy any stock including sector ETFs and sector funds. This book provides a simple chart to detect market plunges. Basically it is a sector rotation between SPY (an ETF that simulates the market) and cash (or an ETF of short-term bonds).

- The next rotation strategy involves four ETFs in a rising market described in Chapter 4. Optionally, you can include a contra ETF to time the market. Buy the best performer of last month of the selected ETFs.

- Some sectors perform better in different stages of a market cycle.

- Many free sites describe the best sector performers such as Seeking Alpha and CNNfn.

- Evaluate sector using Technical Analysis and Fundamental Analysis. Use the same tools to evaluate individual stocks within a performing sector – top-down investing.

- You should spend one hour or two a month to determine which sector to rotate to or move your portfolio to cash when the market is risky. The "Buy and hold" strategy does not perform since 2000.

- Subscription services. There are many. Even if you subscribe these services, you should read this book to evaluate their services and use this book as a second opinion. When your portfolio is over $100,000, $100 for a yearly subscription should pay itself in the long run.

- Market timing by calendar and presidential cycle.

- My recent experiences in sector trading.

- Be careful on many books on this topic were written by professors who may never make a buck in the stock market.

- Some "best" sellers were written more than 10 years ago that do not have today's basic tools such as technical analysis and bear any resemblance to today's market, which can be manipulated by institution investors.

- Most large companies today are global companies. The importance in investing foreign companies to diversify is less important than before.

- When China expands, natural resource-rich countries would most likely benefit.

- Most similar books have one strategy and this book has 11 strategies. You can combine the strategies such as market timing with last month's best-performed sector.

Besides industrial sectors, I include bonds, contra ETFs, sector mutual funds, countries, commodities, etc. Today, most sectors are covered by ETFs. For example, you do not need to buy gold coins to invest in that sector but the ETF GLD.

Sectors

The primary sectors are: Basic Materials, Consumer Discretionary, Consumer Staples, Energy, Financial, Health Care, Industrial, Technology and Utilities. Click the links or search from Wikipedia for description of these sectors.

https://www.fidelity.com/sector-investing/overview

We can sub divide a sector into industries. For example, Technology can be divided into Computer and Software. Some industries such as banking software can cross more than one sector.

The above links describe sectors pretty good by Fidelity with the exception of Technology, which is divided into several sectors such as Software, Computer and Telecom by Fidelity. Here are my views on the major sectors.

Consumer Staples and Discretionary

Consumer Staples are food, beverages, household products and the products we buy as necessity. They are recession-proof. The US products have demonstrated high quality and safety. With the growing middle class in developing countries such as China and India, we expect they should grow outside the USA. Currently it is not due to tariffs.

Consumer Discretionary are just the opposite.

Sector Timing

During a recession some sectors such as Consumer Staples and Health Care work better than other sectors such as Technology. They will be opposite from above during the go-go era when consumers have more money to buy non-essential goods and companies have money to invest.

Some sectors are more volatile than others. Some sectors such as Health Care would benefit by the growing or aging global population.

Sectors	Major Industries	Favorable
Basic Materials	Metals, Mining, Chemicals	High inflation / Growing economy
Consumer Discretionary	Auto, Building, High-end Retail	Low interest rate
Consumer Staples	Food	Recession
Energy	Oil, Gas, Exploration	Growing economy
Industrial	Machines	Economic recovery
Health Care	Delivery, Drugs, Biotech	Recession for Delivery
Financial	Bank, Insurance	High interest, Growing economy
Technology	Computer, software	Growing economy
Utilities	Electricity, Gas	Recession

A list of sectors.
http://www.investorguide.com/sector-list.php

6 Strategies that worked before

The following are three popular strategies that worked before but not too well recently. I try to see whether I can revive them to return to their former glory.

1. O'Shaughnessy's Strategy
(http://en.wikipedia.org/wiki/James_O%27Shaughnessy)

It made a stunning return from 1954 through 1994. His strategy is:

Buy the 50 DOW stocks that have the highest one-year returns, five consecutive years of rising earnings and share prices less than 1.5 times their corporate rate revenues.

After he publicized his strategy in a book, it is no longer effective. It is his tradeoff to make a lot of money from his book and his personal prestige to making money in his mutual funds. It fits my saying: When too many folks follow the same strategy, it will no longer be useful.

2. The Foolish Four
(http://en.wikipedia.org/wiki/Foolish_Four)

From Wikipedia: "The "Foolish Four" is a discredited[1] mechanical investing technique that, like the Dogs of the Dow, attempts to select the member stocks of the Dow Jones Industrial Average that will outperform the average in the near future.

To identify the "Foolish Four," an investor determines the current dividend yield and current price for each of the 30 stocks comprising the Dow Jones Industrial Average. Then, the yield for each stock is divided by the square root of the stock's price. The stocks are ranked from highest to lowest using the number resulting from the division. The stocks ranking the second highest, third highest, fourth highest, and fifth highest in equal dollar amounts are bought. The highest ranking stock is not bought."

3. Buy the highest ROE stocks

It has been described in a popular book. I do not believe it still works but the book is still popular. I do not think I can revive this strategy and it is NOT the Holy Grail in investing as blindly followed by many. The followers should replace this strategy with better strategies.

My take

The above three strategies work at one time. After the authors publicized their strategies, they did not work anymore.

The ROE strategy will not work consistently as it is only one of the many fundamental metrics the value investor should consider. The Foolish Four seems to be similar to the Dog of Dows. Hence, the only serious modification is on O'Shaughnessy's strategy.

Modify O'Shaughnessy's Strategy

I would take another look at O'Shaughnessy's Strategy. It is a long-term momentum strategy with some protection of not buying over-priced stocks. It will be effective again when fewer folks use it. Check its current performance. Many stock screens such as AAII's simulate this strategy. The following modifications apply to similar screens for this strategy.

What to include:

- Include S&P 500 stocks, so you have more stocks to select besides the Dow stocks.
- Alternatively, include stocks in all three major exchanges.
- Optionally select stocks with prices greater than $2 (or $5 for conservative investors), and daily average volumes greater than 10,000 shares. It would effectively eliminate most penny stocks.
- Use the expected earnings which predicts better instead of the last twelve month's earnings.
- Skip the stocks from most if not all emerging foreign countries (at least for today).
- Score each stock fundamentally such as using my Scoring System described in my books. Discard all the stocks that do not pass the scoring system.
- Analyze each stock fully.

Timing:

- Buy in November 1 and sell in May 1 for retirement accounts; alternatively start buying in October 15 and sell in April 15 for better choices and avoid the herd.
- Buy in November and December for non-retirement accounts to avoid the crowd. Sell losers after holding them less than a year and winners over a year in non-retirement accounts. Long-term capital gains have better tax treatments - check the current tax laws for both Federal and the state you reside in.
- When the market has a high chance to plunge or is plunging, close out all positions.
- Consider covered calls on stocks that are qualified for lower long-term capital gain taxes.

Optimal number of stocks:

- If you cannot find enough stocks to buy, relax your selection criteria such as 3 consecutive years of rising earnings instead of 5 years. If you still cannot find many good stocks, it could mean the market is fully valued and / or there are few bargains. It could also be due to too many folks following the same strategy.
- If you find too many stocks, sort them in descending order of the expected yields (E/P) and select the top stocks. Omit stocks with

yields higher than 35% as they may sound fishy for such high returns. Alternatively, consider the stocks with high scores in my scoring system.

- 50 stocks is too large a number for most retail investors. Cut it to 25 (and even 10 if you have less than $50,000 to invest). Ensure that there is no sector having its total value more than 25% of the portfolio for better diversification.

Adjust the strategy to your risk tolerance and requirements. If you do not have a lot of time, five stocks in different sectors should be diversified enough.

Paper test the strategy before you commit with real money. If you have a historical database, test it and tune it for better result.

Filler: Happy Mother's Day Poem

(This is my translation from an unknown Chinese author)

I cried at two unforgettable times in my life.

The first time when I came to this world.
The second time when you left this world.

The first time I did not know but from your mouth.
The second time you did not know but from my heart.

Between these two crises, we had endless laughs.
But for the last 30 years, we had joyful laughs that had been repeated, repeated...

You treasured every laugh.
I remember every laugh for the rest of my life.

7 *The best strategy*

It is Buy Low and Sell High.

It is simple but most retail investors just do the opposite: Buy High and Sell Low. The flow of money to/from money market funds turns out to be a reliable contrary indicator.

The Early Recovery in 2003 and 2009 and the later part of June, 2012 could be the best time to buy.

The above represents buy at low prices and sell at high prices. Considering P/E (positive 'E' only), buy at low P/E of a stock, a sector and the market (via an ETF) and sell them respectively at high P/E.

Here are some hints when to buy and sell with this strategy:

- Sell when everyone including your silly mother-in-law is making good money and all participants think they're financial geniuses. It could be the riskiest time. The high interest rate (my yardstick is over 5% for Fed Discount rate, the best rate the Fed lends to the banks) usually confirms this as folks falsely expect better return even they pay more on interest to borrow money to buy stocks.

- Do not buy the stocks that were the bubble-forming stocks such as the technology stocks in 2001-2002 and the bank stocks in 2008-2009 as some 'optimists' think it is time to return and usually they're wrong.

  Do not think the stock is a good deal when it loses half of its value. Buy them only when the root problem has been fixed. The best time to return to the market after a market plunge is usually two years after the market plunge (2003 for the market plunge in 2000 and 2009 for the market plunge in 2007/2008). Many bubble stocks never recover and many of these stocks take more than 3 years to recover. Their prices appear to be low, but no one can predict the bottom unless it goes to zero.

- Be careful on the sector or group of stocks that have winning streak for more than two years. Most likely they will correct. Use stop loss to protect your profits if you want to keep them.

  You could have saved a lot if you use this strategy on tech stocks in 2000. As of 2015, dividend stocks could be the next sector to burst but only time can tell. Do not fall in love with a stock. Yesterday's winners could be tomorrow's losers, and vice versa.

  'Buy and hold' is dead since 2000. We have two market plunges with an average loss of about 45% from their peaks.

- Do not buy dividend stocks solely for their dividends. Most of them are matured companies; most have less growth and hence less appreciation potential. They usually lose less value in a recession after dividends. Income investors are chasing them for higher dividends than bonds.

  Except from Roth accounts, when you withdraw from your retirement accounts, your dividends will be treated as income. Check the current tax rates for income and dividend from taxable accounts.

- Buy value stocks that seem to be bottomed. It is hard to identify the bottom. When the appreciation potential outweighs the risk, it could be a buy.

- Buy the stocks that have been losing money but their burn rates can last for the entire recession. They're risky but the potential profits are great. There were many in 2003 and 2009. Even in a bad economy in 2012, a few corporations had historically low P/Es.

- Buy against the experts who have unconvincing predictions. They usually exaggerate the rosy outlooks of the companies in order to sell the stocks they own. This is one of the few times you should bet against them. Use your better judgment to ensure how false their predications are.

- No one can predict consistently the market bottom. However, use your better judgment with educated guesses to gain an edge. Refer to the exit point using the 350-day SMA from the chapter on detecting market plunges.

Using Citicorp (symbol C) as an example

Following the chapter on avoiding bank stocks, buying this stock at $550 a share could be avoided. After the big plunge in 2008, I believe it has long- term profit potential. Accumulate this stock if you believe C will be profitable in 10 years (2024) or so. Do not sell it unless there is potential for a market plunge. If so, buy it back after the plunge. One's opinion.

With our market timing (defending sector may return in two years), I checked it in mid 2009, about 2 years after the start of the market plunge. Optionally I could use the SMA-350 of the stock to determine the reentry point. However, it had no meaning due to the big plunge from $550. On 8/2009, C's P/E was negative, so I did not buy it.

Alternatively buy it for every big drop in P/E regardless of the current price as follows. We started when the P/E is about 40. Normally I buy it when the P/E is at around 20. Take an exception for turnaround stocks.

Date	P/E	Price
06/2010	40	40
01/2011	13	49
08/2011	9	32

The above is for illustration only, so the numbers are not precise.

As of 6/12/2014, I expected a correction, so I sold it at about $48. I only trade this kind of stocks when I see long-term appreciation potential. The other three important metrics are P/B, P/S and RSI(14). Use forward (expected) P/E if possible. The most important metric for lenders is the quality of the loans, which is hard to evaluate for retail investors. The other factor is any serious, pending lawsuits. When Lehman Brothers was gone, the governments will chase after the institutions that sold the derivatives.

The second best strategy

Buy high and sell higher.

When everyone is looking for stocks with the highest value, there may not be any such stocks available. It seems to contradict with my best strategy but it is not. Fundamentals may not show everything about the company such as a new drug, a new product... The all-time high prices usually show that. Buy the stock when it is over the 50-day simple moving average (50 or 200 days depending on how long you usually hold a stock) via finviz.com.

Buying fully-priced stocks is dangerous even it may be profitable. To protect your profits:

- Be extra careful in risky market; I prefer not to buy any stock when the market is risky.

- Set stop loss orders. Recommend 10% (or 15% for volatile stocks) less than the current price. If you set 5% stop, it would be stopped out for normal fluctuations.

- Use Technical Analysis. When the price drops below the moving average you used, sell it. When RSI (14) is high (over 70), check out the reason as it could be overbought.

If you are not very sure, sell half of it. You will not get broke for taking profits.

As in life, there are no guarantees, but using a proven technique / discipline is far better than trading without one. Paper trading to ensure the strategy fits the current market conditions, your personal tolerance and requirements.

The third best strategy

Buy very high and sell even higher.

It is the riskiest. These stocks could be bubble stocks moved by institution investors and then moved even higher by retail investors. It may take a while before the institution investors rotate to another sectors / stocks and/or take profit.

My strategy is to follow the herd but ensure you're ready to exit.

- Identify them. Usually they are large caps with high trade volumes.

- Do not short them.

- Buy them ignoring the fundamentals as they are moved up with the herd sometimes for a reason and sometimes not. Alternatively, use options.

- Set mental stop losses. Adjust the stops periodically after they appreciate.

- Watch them every day. Bring up Finviz.com and enter the sector ETF the stock belongs to and the stocks. Pay attention to SMA200%: The higher it is, the higher chance it is peaking. When RSI(14) is over 70% (65% for sectors), most likely it is overbought.

Super safe strategies

These strategies are for orphans and widows. The common theme is that you want to spend little time in investing. There are better things to do than investing. You may not have the knowledge in investing or the desire to learn investing. However, most likely the safe strategies do not beat inflation except the last strategy described in this article.

Strategy #1: CD and long-term treasury bills

They are virtually risk-free. Even it is almost no-effort strategy except in renewing the expired CDs, I still recommend some actions:

- Do not invest in a CD with a bank that you have already exceeded the government's limit in insurance. As of 2016, the standard deposit insurance coverage limit is **$250,000** per depositor, per FDIC-insured bank and per ownership category.
- Today's CDs do not beat inflation. It is our capitalist system that punishes us for not taking risk and effort in investing.

- Some mortgage-backed bonds or similar offerings could lose all the value as many found out the hard way from Lehman Brother's bonds disguised as safe CDs.
- Buy long-term treasury bills when the interest rate is high (say 5% or higher). Buy short-term treasury bills when the interest rate is low (say less than 2%). Although you can receive your entire principle plus interest when they mature, the value of the bond fluctuates in opposite direction to the current rate. When the current interest rate is better than the one in your treasury bill, your bill will depreciate.
- Most folks buy the treasury bills via mutual funds and/or ETFs.

Strategy #2: Annuity

When you retire, it seems to be a good vehicle to buy an annuity to provide income for life. However, you have to understand the annuities' terms are defined by the sellers with their own agenda. If you believe they're in business to make you a comfortable retirement at their own expenses, think again. Very few if any are low-expense operations. Ask how much the salesman would make to sell you the annuity, and most likely you would run to the door for quick exit.

I invested in annuity when I was working to postpone my taxes for the gains. It could be a mistake for me even I made over 4 times during several decades. My taxes after 70 ½ (the age for mandatory withdrawal of retirement accounts) will be higher than my working years. I did well in rotating sectors (offered in my annuity) partly due to luck. The total expenses (the trading fees and the management fees) are not cheap compared to most ETFs.

It is good when you have better things to do in your life than worrying about the market. It would save some taxes if your tax bracket is lowered after retirement (as most folks do). If we have a market plunge, then these two strategies would be winner.

Strategy #3: Rotation of an ETF and cash

Rotate between SPY (or any ETF that stimulates the market) and cash (or a short-term treasury bond ETF). When the market is risky, rotate your investment into cash and vice versa for SPY. This book describes market timing; it is quite simple.

For beginners, it appears more complicated than it is. You only spend several minutes every month. You will beat most mutual fund managers as most of them are not allowed to play market timing. To start, allocate a small percentage of your investing to this strategy or test the strategy on paper. There is some risk due to false signals. However, "nothing risk, nothing gained" is quite true especially for the long term.

Section VII: Market timing on market crashes

The apples you picked are sour but some other times are tasty from the same tree. You just pick them in the wrong time or in the right time. It is nothing wrong with the tree but timing.

Market timing is about educated guesses unless you have a time machine. Hopefully we will have more rights than wrongs when we follow general guidelines. It would reduce risk and could benefit us financially in the long run.

I divide the market timing in three categories by durations as follows. All time durations are estimates.

1. Secular Cycle. Duration: 20 years.
2. Market Cycle. Duration: 5 years.
3. Correction. Duration: 1/2 for 5% and 1 yr. for 10%.

---

1 The power of market timing

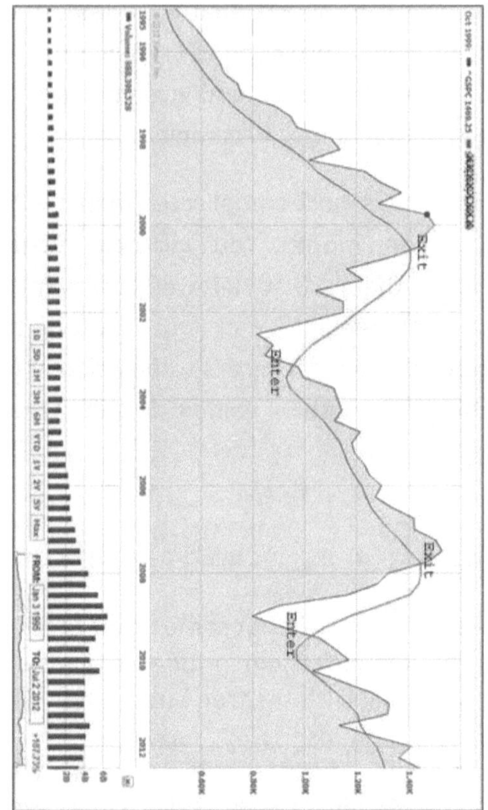

Most e-book readers allow you to select the graph to make it fit entirely on your screen. I use SPY, an ETF simulating the market. Detecting market plunges as seen in this graph indicates the exit points and reentry points also from 2000 to 9-2009 as follows.

Market Plunge	Peak	Bottom	Indicator Exit	Indicator Reenter
2000	08/28/00	09/20/02	10/01/00	06/01/03
2007	10/12/07	03/06/09	02/01/08	09/01/09
			08/01/11	11/01/11

Table: Vital Dates

For simplicity I skipped a few brief exits and reentries since 2011. You can run the simple chart once a month. When it indicates a potential market plunge is close, run the chart once a week. The last row represents a false signal.

This is based on stock prices so it may not identify the peaks and bottoms precisely, but so far it has not failed to avoid big losses and ensure big gains by reentering the market. I hope the next market plunge would give us enough time to act as these two did.

Unbelievable return with market timing

Calculate how much you made if you followed the above exit points and reenter points from 2000 to today. I bet you would have made a good fortune.

I compared the above returns with the SPY without market timing from 1-2000 to 9-2013.

There are many assumptions. Dividends and compounding are not considered. My return should be substantially better if I include buying contra ETFs during the exits and selling them during the reentries. I was shocked by the incredible return by using this simple market timing. Again, past performance does not guarantee future performances.

Summary info:

S&P 500 1-2000 to 9-2013	With Market Timing	Without Market Timing
Better	**500%**	
Gain	1,000	167
Gain %	68%	11%
Annualized gained	5%	1%
Days	4,959	4,959

Calculations:

S & P 500	With Market Timing	Without Market Timing
1-2000	1,469[1]	1,469[1]
Exit 10/01/00	1,041[2]	1,041
Enter 06/01/03	1,041	964[4]
Exit 02/01/08	1,489[3]	1,379[4]
Enter 09/01/09	1489	1,020[5]
Exit 08/01/11	1,888	1,293
Enter 11/01/11	1,888	1,251
09/03/13	2,469	1.638
Gained	2,469 – 1,469=1,000	1,638-1,469=167
Gain %	1000/1469 = 68%	167/1469 = 11%
Annualized gained	68% * 365/4959=5%	11%*365/4959=1%
Better	(1,000-167)/167 = 500%	

Portfolio with Market Timing:

[1] Both start with S&P 500 of 1,469 on 1-3-2000.
[2] 10/01/00
The market timing portfolio exits the market and remains the same value of 1,041 until 6/1/00.
[3] 02/01/08
The market timing portfolio exits the market and remains the same value of 1,489 until 9/1/09.

'1,489' is calculated as follows:
1,041 * (1 + Rate) = 1,041 * (1 + 1,379-964)/964) = 1,489
where the S&P 500 is 964 on 6/1/00 and 1,379 on 2/1/08.

The other calculations are based on the S&P 500 at 1,020 on 9/1/9, 1,293 on 8/1/11, 1,251 on 11/1/11 and 1,636 on 9/3/13.

Portfolio without Market Timing:

[1] Both starts with the S&P 500 of 1,469 on 1-3-2000. We could use the 9/3/13 the S&P 500 value, but it would not account for some compounded interest considerations.

[4] S&P 500 is 964 on 6/1/00 and 1,379 on 2/1/08.

[5] 02/01/08. The portfolio value is calculated to be 1,020 as follows:
1,379 * (1 + Rate) = 1,379 * (1 + (1020-1379)/1379) = 1,020
where S&P 500 is 1,379 on 2/1/08 and 1,020 on 9/1/09.

The other calculations are based on the S&P 500 at 1,293 on 8/1/11, 1,251 on 11/1/11 and 1,636 on 9/3/13.

I cannot believe the shocking return with market timing. I checked my calculations and there was nothing wrong that I could find.

Market timing example

The market is making new highs. There are always two camps of market timers. One camp predicts a crash is coming while the other predicts it will continue making new highs. This article includes both arguments and suggests how and what actions you need to take to protect your investments.

Management summary

The market is fundamentally unsound evidenced by fundamental metrics but technically sound evidenced by technical metrics that both will be described in this article. The data were obtained on 09/22/2018. The market has not changed a lot as of 01/2020.

Suggested actions
No one predicts the market correctly and consistently. Otherwise there are no poor folks. Moving the risky investments such as most stocks to cash too early would miss the potential profits. Moving it too late would risk the loss of your stocks.

Your actions depend on your risk tolerance. If you are conservative such as a retiree, you may want to have a larger portion of your investments in lower risk such as CDs and bonds. You can take one of the following three actions or combine all of the three actions.

1. When the market turns to technically unsound, it is time to move your stocks to cash. The market timing indicators may give false signals. In this case, the indicator would tell you to move back to stocks. Most likely you do not lose much except dealing with the consequences of taxes in non-retirement accounts.
2. Move a portion of your risky investments into cash, laddered CDs and/or short-term bonds. Again, the size of the portion depends on your risk tolerance.
3. Use stops. The sell orders would be changed to market orders when the stocks dip below prices specified by you. I prefer to use SPY or other ETF to determine the market direction. Some sectors and some stocks move faster than others. In one crash, my energy stocks were still profitable while the market was tanking. Eventually these energy stocks caught up and fell fast. Today's highly profitable stocks are FAANG stocks as a group.

I propose and prefer ‘manual stop orders’ to prevent market manipulation. However, usually large ETFs cannot be manipulated easily. Manipulators try to profit from your stop orders. Set a stop order price in your `mind. When the stock falls to that specified price, sell it via a market order.

My friend confirmed my “manual stop order”:

“High-frequency trading via Algo Trading Strategy can see exactly where pre-set trailing stops are and sweep across them (play them) like strings on a violin. Pre-set a trailing stop and it is bound to be triggered because Algo hunt them down. Then watch the market rip higher.”

Analysis: Fundamentals and Technical

It consists of Fundamental Analysis and Technical Analysis. The former measures how expensive the current market is and the latter measures the trend of the market.

Many metrics were obtained from Finviz.com as of 9/22/2018 while others are obtained from other websites. With the exception of Fidelity.com, all websites described here are free and readily available. It also serves as a guide on how you can do your own market timing especially after a few months.

The following chart uses SPY to represent the market of the top 500 stocks. It is market cap weighted. It means the higher the market cap the stock, the higher percent of the stock is represented in the index. It turns out most are riskier FAANG stocks.

Enter Finviz.com in your browser and enter SPY. I am not responsible for any errors.

Indicator	**Pass**	**Current Value**	**Indicating**
• Technical			
Death Cross[1]		SMA-50 = 2.3% & SMA-200 = 6.3%	Pass
Technical Analysis: 350 SMA%[2]	>0	Price above the SMA-350.	Pass
RSI(14)	<70	61	Pass
Duration (yr.)	<5	10	Fail
		Overall	**Pass**
• Fundamental			
Valuation			

P/E[3]	<15.7	25.4	High by 62%. Fail.
Shiller P/E[3]	<16.6	33.5	High by 102%. Fail
P/B[3]	<2.78	3.52	High by 27%. Fail.
P/S[3]	<1.50	2.33	High by 55%. Fail.
Oil price	30-100	70.71	Pass
Interest rate[6] T-Bill 1 months[7]	<5	2.05	Pass
T-Bill 3 months[7]	Yield	2.18	
T-Bill 30 years[7]	Curve	3.20	Pass
Flow to Equity[4]		-3.371M	Fail
Flow to bond[4]		7.206M	
Corporate debt/GDP[8]	<40	45%	High by 13%. Fail.
USD[5]		Strong	Fail
Gold		High	Fail
Bubble		Several	Fail
Market experts		Fear long term	Neutral
Politics		Trump	Fail
Misc.		Trade war	Fail
		Overall	**Fail**

[1] This is the market timing technique without using a chart.
[2] I tried to use SMA-400% to reduce false signals without success.
[3] Get it from http://www.multpl.com/ Same as CAPE.
[4] Get it from https://www.ici.org/research/stats. It is based on 09-12-18. "Flow to Equity" is based on domestic ETF estimate. Treat it as two phases in moving to equity. First phase of moving excessively to equity indicates the market is peaking. The second phase indicates the market is plunging when flow of equity is excessively negative.
[5] Global corporations will suffer in profits converted back to USD and hard to sell to foreign countries. [4] Get it from the above link.
[6] Rising interest is bad for corporations and high-ticket products, but good for lenders.

[7] Get it from https://www.treasury.gov/resource-center/data-chart-center/interest-rates/Pages/TextView.aspx?data=yield based on 09/21/18
[8] With the low interest rate, it may not be that critical. Corporations take advantage of the low interest rate.

Overall

Overall, technical is fine as the market is making new highs. Many aggressive investors exit the market on technical indicators only as the over-valued market could linger on for a long term such as from 2009 to 2017 so far.

Overall, fundamental is not sound. The increasing market price also is decreasing the fundamental metrics such as P/E, P/B and P/S. It is bad unless there is reason to support such as the fast earnings growth in 2009.

Many metrics are deteriorating

RSI(14) is getting closer to 65 (a passing grade specified by me).

Inverse yield curve (1.5 vs. 2.33) is about 61% apart from my interpretation and calculation. It is not a warning now but we should keep an eye on it. Most market crashes have occurred when it is 0% or negative. The theory is that in a normal case the short-term interest rates should be lower than the long-term interest rate.

Another source calculates it is 1.1% and that is very close to inversion since the last recession. From MarketWatch, the 30-year fixed interest rates is 4.66% and 1-year rate is 3.96% giving an inverse yield curve 18% apart, which is quite alarming.

Mathematically incorrect, today's full employment is at 4%. Most recessions are closely preceded by troughs in unemployment and the reverse for economy recovery.

GDP growth has been predicted from 1.8% to 3%. The 3% is from the White House for their obvious purpose. I predict it will pop up due to meeting the tariff deadlines, tax cuts and spending increases. It will then be declining to 2%. A healthy US economy should maintain 3% without special factors such as excessive immigration.

We have record debts: investors' margin, corporate debt and Federal debt. These are bubbles going to burst. Federal debt / GDP is about 95% (https://fred.stlouisfed.org/series/gfdegdq188S) today. It does not predict the market performance as this ratio was 53% and 55% before the last two market crashes. It will affect the long-term performance of the economy when we have to service the huge national debt.

We do have 10 years of stock growth at the expense of record Federal deficit. Thanks to President Obama from investors and no thanks from next generations who have to pay back our national debt. It is overdue for a correction. Hopefully it is not a crash which has an average loss of about 45%. We did have two recent corrections losing more than 10%: 2011-12 EU debt crisis and 2014-16 oil crash. The oil price has been rising from $30 per barrel to today's $70. It is still a long way from my warning of $120.

Potential triggers
Trade wars with China, Canada or EU will be the strongest trigger. Our most profitable companies are virtually all international companies. They need fair trade to prosper.

The other trigger is the possible impeachment of President Trump.

Check the validity of our charts
It seems some metrics vary. It could use after hour trading. It could be the "Days" may be "Sessions" – calendar day is different from trading session. I selected 10 years for most of the charts and StockCharts let me select only 5 years.

Here is a list of sites for charts.
https://www.stocktrader.com/2013/12/10/best-free-stock-chart-websites/
These are the three sites I use a lot: Fidelity (customers only), StockCharts and Finviz.com (missing some metrics).

As stated before, SPY may not be the best to represent the market. I prefer an ETF for 1,000 stocks and weigh the stocks evenly (i.e. not according to the market cap). Google "market timing 2020 (or current year)" for more expert info. Here is one.

Mid-year (6/15/2020) update

This is an update to my two articles: "Market timing example" and "Disaster of 2020".

Basically nothing significant has changed recently: The market is fundamentally unsound and technically sound after the recent rally. The only update is our national debt is skyrocketing. Today's "Debt/GDP" is similar to the market height in 2000 and we know what happened afterwards. That's why Buffett has accumulated a lot of cash now.

Even with the unlimited QE (i.e. printing money excessively), the high inflation and market crash predicted by many experts have not been materialized so far. This is my third prediction in "Disaster of 2020". The status of USD as a reserve currency will be shaken; I do not know when, as I do not have a time machine.

Why the market keeps going up while the economy is going down? The Fed has provided a lot of cash and the cash is chasing a fixed number of assets such as gold and stocks. It is the simple, proven theory of demand and supply. It will continue for a while as long as there is unlimited supply of money. At some point, it will pop. At that time, it could lead to a long recession, unless the economy improves as it did in 2009. The smart Fed chairman knows how it will harm the country by excessively printing money. However, he has to obey his boss who is seeking for reelection.

I expect we are in a prolonged period of low interest rates and even negative interest rates. When the rates are negative, our Treasury bonds are no longer marketable. The foreign central banks including China would dump our national debts if it has not been already started. The economy is dressed up nicely in an election year. Giving us free money is the easy way to buy votes, but the long-term effects are very harmful.

Using cheap money to buy back the company's stock would boost the stock price and hence make the management wealthier. It is a false sense of the stock value. When the company cannot pay back the debt obligations, the company would go bankrupted. If the U.S. were a company, she has gone bankrupted already.

As of 6/15/2020, QQQ (representing NASDAQ stocks) has been up 11% YTD and it is far better than DIA (representing DOW stocks) and SPY (representing the 500 large stocks in the S&P Index and losing about 5% YTD). QQQ has a lot of tech stocks while DIA has a lot of losers including Boeing. Most FAANG stocks are making record highs and QQQ is market cap weighed.

Most of the ETFs on chips have been up more than 40% in a year. I bought Amazon and two chip ETFs. I use trailing stops to protect my portfolio. Huawei is buying a lot of U.S. chips in the 120-day relaxed period. In September this year and if there is no extension, I would sell these chip ETFs fast.

I have used the strategy described in my book "Profit from the recovery of the pandemic" to take advantage of this volatile market. I used 5% as the threshold and I had too few trades; now I changed to 3%. Expecting a market crash, I weigh more on contra ETFs. As described in the same book, I bought a lot of contra ETFs, GLD and the stock of a gold miner. It is for insurance. ETFs on oil is my big mistake.

If the U.S.D. loses the status of reserve currency (not likely soon), it would bring prolonged depression and high inflation in the U.S. In this case, it is safer to invest in real estate, precious metals and profitable companies than in CDs and bonds that would lose values due to inflation.

Check out many articles on the status of the current market. Many have opposing views, so you have to make your own decision. In any case, play it safe with stops. Here is one article from MarketWatch.com.

3 Market cycle

"Bull markets are born on pessimism, grow on skepticism, mature on optimism, and die on euphoria" - Sir John Templeton

The stock market has cycles as our practical interpretation of the above. It is about five years apart, but it fluctuates widely. I divide it into four stages: Bottom, Early Recovery, Up and Peak.

My defined four stages of a market cycle

We need to apply the right investing strategies to each of the four stages of the cycle.

- **Bottom**

  I would not invest for at least the first six months (or even a year) after the big plunge starts, which could lose over 25% in a few months. The exceptions are investing in contra ETFs and selling short for aggressive investors.

  I estimate it will take a year from the start of the plunge to the bottom, so I will normally sell stocks early in the plunge and do not buy stocks that are in the sector (sometimes sectors) that causes the bubble for about two years after the plunge.

  At the bottom, the high-yield corporate bonds (i.e. junk bonds) would prosper when the interest rates is decreasing to stimulate the economy.

  From mid-2007 to mid-2008, bonds suffered as the investors thought the sky was falling down - it was to those who lost the jobs and/or their houses. After that, some bonds especially the long-term bonds appreciated about 50% for the following year.

  The government lowered the interest rates and these bond prices with high interest rates surged. Correct timing in buying bonds could be very profitable.

  Long-term bonds have more impact by the interest rate: The lower the interest rate, the higher the bond prices of higher-yield bonds. The older bonds with higher interest rates are more valuable to the newer bonds with lower interest rates.

I define this period of the bottom from the start of the plunge to the start of Early Recovery.

- **Early Recovery**
  It usually starts after one year from the plunge; no one can pin point the exact time consistently. By this time preferably earlier, we should have closed out all positions in contra ETFs and shorts.

  Roughly speaking, October, 2007 (some use 2008) is the start of the market plunge. March, 2009 is the end of the bottom stage and the start of the early recovery stage of the 2007 cycle. However, every market cycle is different in where it starts and ends.

  The one-year gain from the bottom is most profitable. It usually gains over 25% in a year from the market bottom. I, a conservative investor, had huge gains using some leverage in my largest taxable account in 2009. From my memory, I had a similar return in 2003 but I had not saved the statement as in 2009.

  In this phase, value is a better parameter than growth in searching for stocks. If your investment subscription provides a composite value score and a composite timing score, the sort parameter of your screened stocks could be "Composite Value / Composite Timing" in descending order. Select the top stocks in this order. You still have to analyze the top-screened stocks.

  Forward (same as Expected) P/E is a good metric. However, most companies may be losing money at this stage. Those companies that can last for more than one year with its cash reserve are potential good buys. The best appreciated stocks are beaten companies that have precious technologies and good customer bases. They could be candidates to be acquired if they are small enough.

- **Up**

Usually the growth metrics such as PEG could be better than the value metrics such as expected P/E during this phase. Most stocks are winners except contra ETFs and shorting stocks. When the growth stocks are making headlines and the defensive stocks are being dumped, this is the hint that we're well into the Up phase of the market cycle.

Locate stocks with growth metrics such as favorable PEG and high SMA-200% (from Finviz.com). Do not be scared on how much they have already appreciated. The strategy "Buy High and Sell Higher" works in this phase. Protect your profits with stops.

Ensure that they have value too. Skip the stocks with expected P/Es higher than 35 unless there are good reasons. Most stocks will gain due to the tide of the market. However, when they're overbought (RSI(14) over 60), be careful. When institutional investors sell these stocks, they will crash.

- **Peak**
  When everyone makes easy money and the interest rates is high, watch out. Stop loss and/or stop limit should be used to protect your investment. Check out whether there is any bubble that would be burst like the internet in 2000 and the finance (and housing) in 2007.

  Internet crisis is easy to spot, but not the financial crisis. In 2007 we had a cycle longer than the average which is about 5 years. The plunge is very fast and very steep – thanks to the institutional investors who drive the market down.

  Run the technical analysis chart described in the Chapter on Spotting Big Market Plunges at least monthly (weekly if you have time). Protect your investment. Do not fall in love with any stock (you can buy it back later at a deep discount). Making the last buck is a fool's game.

  Accumulate cash according to your risk tolerance. A retiree or a conservative investor would accumulate from 25% to 50% and should be ready to move to all cash when the plunge starts.

  We can lower the cash percent if we use enough stop loss protection. Be psychologically prepared because the stock market may still rise for a while. There is no perfect market timing.

The 2007 Cycle

The market plunged starting in 10-2007 and ending in 3-2009 (bottom), started to recover in 3-2009 (early recover), and trended up from 2010 to 1-2013 (the up phase of the market cycle). As of 3/2016, it is the peak phase defined by me.

As of 1/2013, we have recovered all the market losses since 2007. However, as of 7/2014, the economy has not fully recovered compared to the economy before the plunge. The employment judging by the medium salary has not fully recovered and the economy is not expanding. It is uncommon that the economy does not follow the market. It is due to the excessive supply of money by the government and partly due to globalization to allow companies to hire overseas.

Although a W-shaped recession seldom happens, we have a chance today. We hope we do not have a depression and/or the similar lost decades that Japan has been experiencing. Some may conclude we are close to completing a market cycle from 2007 to 2016. As of 2016, the economy is recovering slowly and we're better than most other global economies.

Again, market timing is not an exact science as it involves irrational human beings and government interventions. The timing using market cycle described here is a guideline as it is hard to time it exactly.

The average market cycle is about 5 years, but they fluctuate. If we consider 2007 as the plunge, we have about 8 years of this cycle as of 2015.

In a typical cycle (few are typical), we have about one year in each of the 4 phases I defined (plunge, early recovery, up and peak).

Events/Triggers

There are financial events and triggers that cause the transition of one phase of the market cycle to another. They usually do not change the sequence of the phases (say not from Peak to Early Recovery), but they may change the duration of the phase. Examples are:

- The government announcing change of the interest rate,
- Change of employment, and
- Change of GNP.

Sectors in a market cycle (my suggestion)

Market Phase	Favorable		Unfavorable
Early Recovery	Financial, Technology, Industrial		Energy, Telecom, Utilities
Up	Technology, Industrial, Housing		
Peak	Mineral, Health Care, Energy, Long-Term Bond, Consumer Discretionary		
Bottom	Consumer Staples, Utilities		Consumer Discretionary, Technology, Industrial, Long-Term & high-yield Bond

The sectors that cause the recession usually take a longer time to recover. In 2000, the technology sector was not favorable in the Early Recovery phase, contrary to the above table. In 2007, the financial sector was not favorable in the Early Recovery phase. These are the "offending" sectors that cause the plunges.

In a recession, we usually cannot cut down on consumer staples and utilities, but we can cut down on buying consumer gadgets. Companies usually postpone investing in equipment and systems during a recession and expand when the economy is humming. The government usually lowers the interest rates right after the plunge to stimulate the economy.

Conclusion

When the market is about to plunge or change from one stage to another, run the described chart more frequently and read more articles written by the experts. Again, market timing is not an exact science but it is based on educated guesses. The better guesses should have more rights than wrongs in the long term. Our actions depend on our risk tolerance. Be careful on using any new strategy that has not been fully understood and proven. Since 2000, market timing is very important to your financial health with two market plunges with an average of about 45% loss.

4 Calendar Timing

I made the following charts so it is easier to time the market by calendar. All dates are inclusive.

No.	Metric		Score
1	Seasonal	Nov. - April, Score = 1	
2	Best Month	Nov., Score = 1	
		Sep., Score = -1	
3	Best Days	Dec. 15 – Jan.15 Score = 1	
4	Presidential Cycle	Election Year, Score = 1	
		1st Year in Office, Score = -1	
		2nd year, Score = -1	
		3rd year, Score = 2	
5	Market Cycle[1]	Plunging, Score = -3	
		Early Recovery, Score = 3	
		Up, Score = 2	
		Peak, Score = 1	
		Grand Score	

1 Refer to the Market Cycle chapter on how I define phases of a cycle.

Add up all the scores. The passing grade for the grand score is 1 but I have not really tested out past performance. It is the first time you see a scoring system on market timing combining.

Sectors for market cycle

Market Phase[1]	Favorable		Unfavorable
Early Recovery	Financial, Technology, Industrial		Energy, Telecom, Utilities
Up	Technology, Industrial		
Peak	Mineral, Health Care, Energy		
Bottom	Consumer Staples, Utilities		Consumer Discretionary, Technology, Industrial
Seasonal	**Favorable**		**Unfavorable**
Winter	Energy, Utilities		
End of year	QQQ, EWG		
Olympics	ETF for host country[2]		

1 Refer to Market Cycle chapter on how I define phases of a cycle.
Buy it next year after Olympics. It could be due to higher GDP or the publicity. However, be selective. Greece is too small a country to host an Olympics.

2 Buy it next year after Olympics. It could be due to higher GDP or the publicity. However, be selective. Greece is too small a country to host an Olympics.

Summary

I made the following charts so it is easier to time the market by calendar. All dates are inclusive.

No.	Metric		Score
1	Seasonal	Nov. - April, Score = 1	
2	Best Month	Nov., Score = 1	
		Sep., Score = -1	
3	Best Days	Dec. 15 – Jan.15 Score = 1	
4	Presidential Cycle	Election Year, Score = 1	
		1st Year in Office, Score = -1	
		2nd year, Score = -1	
		3rd year, Score = 2	
5	Presidential[3]	Democratic = 1 Republican = -1	
6	Market Cycle[1]	Early Recovery,	

		Score = 3	
		Up, Score = 2	
		Peak, Score = 1	
7	SPY (Finviz.com)	SMA200% > 8%[2] Score = -1	
		SMA200% < 0 Score = -1	
		RSI(14) > 65% Score = -1	
		Grand Score	

1 Refer to Market Cycle chapter on how I define phases of a cycle.

2 For simplicity, use Finviz.com. Enter SPY and you will find SMA200% and RSI(14) to predict whether the market is peaking and overbought.

3 I'm political neutral. The selection is based on historical statistics.

Add up all the scores. The passing grade is 0. According to my table which is based on my personal selections/preferences, the market is favorable when the grand score is 1 or higher. I bet it is the first time you see such a scoring system for market timing.

Sectors for market cycle

Market Phase[1]	**Favorable**		**Unfavorable**
Early Recovery	Financial, Technology, Industrial		Energy, Telecom, Utilities
Up	Technology, Industrial		
Peak	Mineral, Health Care, Energy		
Bottom	Consumer Staples, Utilities		Consumer Discretionary, Technology, Industrial
Seasonal	**Favorable**		**Unfavorable**
Winter	Energy, Utilities		
End of year	QQQ, EWG		
Olympics	ETF for host country[2]		

1 Refer to Market Cycle chapter on how I define phases of a cycle.

2 Buy it next year after Olympics. It could be due to higher GDP or the publicity. However, be selective. Greece is too small a country to host an Olympics.

5 Politics and investing

You may ask why politics is discussed in this investing book. Politics has been proven to affect the market. For example, the market had reacted to the different stages of Quantitative Easing whose dates had been preset. The following is a more recent example.

I predicted 2015 would be a year with small profit and insisted on so even during the fierce correction in August. Why I was so sure? Very seldom the market is down in a year before an election year including 2007. The last occurrence was 1939, the year when WW2 started. Investing is a multi-discipline venture including statistics and politics. It may not always happen, but the probability is high for these years.

How to profit

2015 was a sideward market. The market reacted to good news and bad news. The strategy for sideway market is: Buy at temporary downs and sell at temporary peaks. Define 'temporary' according to your risk tolerance.

For the 'temporary market down', personally I used 5% down from the last market peak. To me the 'temporary market peak' is 10% up from the last market down. The percentages can apply to the percentage changes in the stocks in your watch list. In another words, I buy the stock when the market is 5% down from the last peak and sell it when it gains 10% or the market gains 10%. Be reminded that this strategy is opposite to market plunges, where you should exit the market totally - again depending on your risk tolerance.

The following are my purchases on 08/26/2015. I should have bought more stocks and one day earlier if I were not blinded by fears (a human nature) during this correction. Here is my proof for my purchase orders. The four stocks were described as value stocks in a SA article and I did a simple evaluation. As of 12/31/2015, I sold all the four stocks except Gilead Sciences. The annualized returns are more impressive such as GNW's 10% gain in one day.

Stocks	Buy Price	Buy Date	Return	Sold date
Apple (AAPL)	107.20	08/26/15	12%	10/19/15
Gilead Sciences (GILD)	105.94	08/26/15	-4%	
General Motors (GM)	27.69	08/26/15	12%	09/17/15
Genwealth Financial (GNW)	4.54	08/26/15	10%	08/27/15

There were similar examples in 2013 and 2014.

2016: Politics and the market

No one including all the Federal Reserve chairmen / chairwomen and all the Nobel-Prize winners in economics can predict market plunges. One chairman predicted a smooth market and a few months later the housing market crashed. Many predicted correctly market crashes by pure luck. One even received a Nobel Prize and became famous. However, you are glad to ignore his later market predictions.

There are at least two best sellers asking us to exit the market in 2009. If you followed them, you would miss all the big gains from 2009 to 2014. They did have a point. However, you cannot fight the Fed. The market had been saved by the excessive printing of money and hence created a non-correlation between the market and the economy. I bet these authors (famous economists and gurus) may have not made a buck in the stock market. It is a classic case of the blind leading the blind.

From their articles, they do not know the basic technical indicator. You only want react to the market when the market is plunging and not too early. That's why most fund managers cannot beat the market as most are not allowed to time the market. Buffett had mediocre returns in the last three years – I had warned my readers three years ago in my blogs/books. To me, the 'buy-and-hold' strategy is dead since 2000. The average loss from the peak for the last two market plunges is about 45%. Most charts depend on falling prices, so you will not save 45% and 25% loss is my objective.

Fundamentally speaking

The market in 2016 is risky due to the proposed interest rates hike, our record-high margin, strong U.S. dollar and the high expenses of the wars to start. Each reason could be a good-size article. Personally I try to maintain 50% in cash and would flee the market if my technical indicator tells me so.

Politically (and statistically) speaking

The election year is the second best for the market, but it may not be this year. We seldom have three terms from the same political party. For that, I predict a win by the Republicans. Republicans are usually pro-business, but ironically the democratic presidency has better track record for better market performance.

The market has more than recovered since the day when Obama took office. The S&P500 performance under Republicans vs. Democrats since 1926 to 2014 is approximately:

Annualized return under Democratic presidencies: 13%
Annualized return under Republican presidencies: 6%

The market is riskier based on the above statistics. In addition, there is a good chance that we will have either a non-politician president or a lady president for the first time. The market usually does not favor to this kind of change.

Critical political issue for 2016

On our way back at about 4 pm on a Saturday, the bus was full of Spanish-speaking workers. I bet most are illegal workers working in my suburb such as our malls, the hospital and many restaurants. Why illegals? I bet most legal folks would get welfare instead of working in that shift. If they work, the state would take away the freebies such as health care in Mass. The illegals do not have this option. I do not think the politicians understand this. There is no need for building a border wall but punishing the employers who hire illegals. Before we do this, we need folks to take the jobs taken by the illegals today.

What will happen if the politicians turn the illegals to be legal?

There will be nobody doing these jobs I predict. No one in the right mind wants these jobs as it is far easier to collect welfare. Why would politicians make this stupid decision? They want to buy Hispanic votes as evidenced in the last two elections.

In addition, most politicians side with the welfare recipients. Since 40% of the population do not pay Federal taxes, the politicians have to satisfy their needs in order to buy votes.

We should encourage folks to work, not the other way round. Representation without taxation is worse than taxation without representation.

Our high taxes, regulations and strong US dollar dampen our competitive edge.

Some political decisions/regulations that affect the stocks

Beside the presidency and the interest rates hike(s), there are many political decisions and regulations that affect the stocks. Just name a few here:

- The never-ending wars postpone our secular bull market beyond 2018.
- Solar City (SCTY). It depends on government energy credit.
- My Chinese solar panel stock evaporated when the US banned them from importing to the US.
- Any gun control measurement will affect gun stocks.
- Restrictions on cigarettes.
- France imposes extra taxes to foreign investors.
- Government bailouts on 'too big to fall' companies.
- Corporate taxes boost the exodus of corporation headquarters to tax heavens for the US. It is the same for Chinese corporations.
- Infrastructure projects.
- Taking out the ban to export oil would increase the profits for oil companies.
- After the annexation of Crimea, the Congress restricted using Russia's rocket engines and gave new opportunity to the US

companies in this area. Besides political consideration, Chinese rockets are the most cost effective and more reliable.

- China's suppressing corruption affected Macau's casinos...

Summary

Politics affect the market. I predict a risky market in 2016. Economy and religion also affect the market. Statistically speaking, the market is ahead of the economy by about 6 months. However, the current market is an exception. The correlation will return to normal.

Religions cause wars as the ones in the Middle East today. These huge expenses are consumption, not investing. It will not be good for most sectors of the economy especially in the long run.

Written in 1/1/2016.

Note.

Predictions are predictions. However, the more the educated the guess is, the better chance the guess will materialize. My technical indicator gave only one false alarm from 2000 to 2009. It happens more often after that period. The market is far more volatile than before. In most cases, false alarms will not hurt at all except tax consequences on taxable accounts. The false alarm tells us to exit the market and come back shortly.

Section: VIII The economy

The economy usually follows the market in six months. However, there are many exceptions and 2013 is one of them.

1 The evils of printing money

I just explained to my grandchild that money does not fall from the sky or grow on trees.

Every time we print money, it does the following:

1. An invisible tax is added to the rich as their purchasing power will be decreased.

2. Your children and grandchildren will pay for it.

3. Selling a piece of our asset to foreigners.

4. Our products are less globally competitive as we have to add more taxes to pay for the loans. It is more competitive initially as our currency has been depreciated, but this will not last long.

5. Give more reasons for the rich to give up citizenship and move to another country. Most become rich for being smart.

6. The end of the USD being a reserve currency is closer.

The only winners are the lobbyists and politicians, who bought votes with the money from your pocket.

It will help the stock market in the short-term, but it is very damaging for the long-term economy. That's also the primary reason why the recovery of our economy is taking forever. Printing money to the maximum is not a solution but a problem.

Afterthoughts

- We have inflation (such as most products in the super market) and deflation (such as housing expenses) since 2008. Click here for detail. http://tonyp4idea.blogspot.com/2012/11/inflation-and-deflation-at-same-time.html

- As of 6/2012, we have 16 trillions of debt and it is substantially less depending on whether you include the entitlements. Besides the poor environment, unpromising economy, our children and grandchildren inherit our huge debts. It is about $55,000 debt for each baby born today. However, many foreigners want their babies born here!

- The U.S. is heading to the same path as Japan by jacking up the money printing press. The similarities are:

  1. Both try to flood the market with free cash. It gives the market a false boost (in nominal term and in after inflation term).

  2. The next generation(s) will have to pay for their citizens' debts.

  3. Both governments are running out of tools to stimulate the market. I guess you cannot have interest rate negative (that means I pay you interest to lend you my money).

  The differences are:

  1. The US has a lot of resources (ores, oil, gas, timber, land, farm land...) per capita and the shale energy could save us for the next 50 years.

  2. The U.S. welcomes immigrants (we need to do it selectively) to reduce some of the demographics problems such as social security, welfare, work force...

  3. Japan will continue another decade of the last two lost decades.

---

2 Low interest rate

As of 2013, we have the lowest interest rates for a long while, which is normal in a recession. It is a great time to buy a house (especially with the depressed house prices) and / or borrow money.

Low interest rates have many impacts on our investment:

- Usually they're better for the stock market as corporations can borrow at cheaper rates and hence improve the bottom line. In theory but not today, it should be great for the housing market and retailers.

- Corporations can borrow money at favorable rates to buy back their own stocks or acquire other companies to boost their own stock prices.

  However, prolonged period of low interest rate will damage the economy. Japan is one example.

- Dividend stocks will prosper from investment on bonds moving to stocks until interest rate starts moving up.

- Folks including retirees, who depend on fix incomes, will suffer.

- Eventually long-term bonds will suffer big time when interest rate moves up.

The government has to lower the rate to stimulate business, but at the same time it cannot prolong the low rate too long.

Afterthoughts

- As of 8/2012, the yield of 10-year Treasury Bill is about 1.75%, the lowest in my recent memory. It is better to keep cash now than CDs, so we do not miss any opportunity to move back to equity.

- Today, we've the lowest interest rate in memory but we're still in a recession; the Fed is running out of tools to improve the economy.

3 Inflation and deflation

The historical annual average is about 3% inflation. CPI is not a good gauge any more after energy and food are not included.

Inflation is:

- An invisible tax to the rich.
- A strategy to lessen the loan burden. To illustrate, your loan of $1 can buy a loaf of bread now, and you will pay back the $1 plus negligible interest that can buy only half a loaf of bread due to inflation. China is the loser and the USA is the winner in this deal.
- An invisible salary cut.
- An invisible cut to your entitlements/welfare. Social security is supposed to be adjusted to CPI, which can be manipulated by the government by not using food and energy to reduce social security payment increases.
- An invisible cut to your investment incomes (dividends and appreciation).

Deflation is no angel:

However, deflation is far worse than inflation to the economy. When the company produces a product and finds out they have to sell it for less due to deflation, then their profit would be cut and they might need to lay off employees.

To illustrate, a manufacturer of making phones calculates the component costs and the expected sell price. If the cost is too high or the profit too low, he would skip the project.

Inflation and deflation at the same time

As of 6/2013, we have both inflation and deflation at the same time for several years now.

We have inflation in most of our basic necessities: food, gasoline and heat (especially important for the NE) with the exception of rent due to the depressed house prices. Electronic stuffs and PCs are deflated considering how much we can buy today vs. last year. Cars have been slightly deflated when figuring in the extra features.

Outlook

The government should ensure inflation and deflation within an acceptable range (3% to me). It has printed a lot of money and lower interest rate to stimulate the economy and at the same time it could have accelerated inflation. When the economy does not improve, it has run out of tools to improve our depressed economy.

However, the shale energy and time would cure all problems.
When the economy is improved, it will accelerate inflation and will also increase the interest rate.

Afterthoughts

- The dollar has lost more than 90% since the FED was created due to inflation. However, it only affects you if you save your cash under the pillow. Our capitalism system punishes those who do not invest and take risk. If you invest in long-term CDs, you're doing barely OK. If you buy any stock such as Edison's new venture or a piece of real estate in your town in 1913, most likely it beats inflation by a good margin and Uncle Sam would glad to share your fortune.

- From my personal experiences.
  The Big Mac Value Meal cost about $1 in 1970 and now it costs $6 – 6 times in 40 years.

  An average house in my hometown in 1980 cost $45,000, and now it costs $450,000 - 10 times in about 30 years.

  Houses in most cases are better deals. Besides paying the tax-deductible property tax and interest, we can live in them.

  The $10,000 under my pillow in 1980 has no gain today, but it gives me a headache every time I sleep on it. ☺

- A bag of 10.5 ounce Lays potato ships is $4.29, and the next day it was downsized it to 9.5 ounces. All items in the grocery store are just like that. The millionaires have no complaint as their stocks (as of 6/2013) have been up and up.

- For those who have jobs, you have a deflation when your same income can buy you more of your basic supplies / services than last year with the exception of food and gasoline.

  Investors' investments are beating the inflation from last year. The wealth gap is widened between the middle class and the rich. Five years ago, the gas price is less than $2 and now it is over $3. We still have high unemployment and high under-employment. Most recent college graduates cannot find jobs or jobs in their choice. It happens all over the world.

- Inflation is controlled by the government via the rate of money being printed and / or easing credit. When we have more money chasing the same quantity of products / services, we have to pay more for them or we call it inflation. In shorter term, it may be distorted by other events such as the deteriorating housing prices.

  With excessive printing, I see hyperinflation in the coming years.

- Inflation is rising.

  Labor

  We have to divide it into two categories: labor that can't be outsourced and labor that can be.

  Labor outsourced to China (your iPhone for example) and India is still relatively cheap.

  Labor in the US like flipping burgers, fixing your plumbing problems, or your telephone services will be increased in cost. If they are not, they will be manipulated by the government via welfare (we pay for them eventually via taxes) or the unions. A worker at Burger King cannot survive without government subsidy or family largesse.

Commodities

All commodities including farm land will increase in value due to:
1. Supply and demand - the net growth of population is rising.

2. Excessive printing of money. You will be able to buy half a loaf of bread with the dollar that used to buy you the full loaf.

- My official definition of Fed in my joke book.
  Fed is an agency to the government, or more like a (selected) mistress to the president. The two are not officially related. But, they're on the same bed most of the day. That's why the president always looks so tired.

  I worked there. Unfortunately I did not climb the corporate ladder all the way otherwise we do not have this economic mess. Same reason the Celtics lose as they did not recruit me.

#Filler: Tip #

As of 3/2014, TSLA, AMAZ, NFLX are all over-priced by any fundamental metrics. However, they are the darlings of institution investors. My advice is not to do anything (not to buy and not to short them) as you cannot fight the city hall.

---

4 The first sip of coffee

Our politicians are 100 times smarter than I, 100,000 times richer than I, handsomer than I (debatable for most esp. Trump)..., why they always made the wrong decisions? Simple answer. Their agenda is buying votes and mine is for the good of our country. Here are the easy fixes.

* Corporate headquarter exodus. Lower their taxes first.

* Health care problem. Lower the medical expenses first.

* Building border walls like the Great Wall of China. Punish the employers who hire the illegals first.

* Social welfare. Do not punish folks for working and give more welfare to workers than those able welfare recipients. It is similar on how to dissolve multi generation of teen-age mothers.

* Fight terrorism. Understand why they want to be one (patriot for them). Think like one on how to give us maximum pain with the least resources.

* Improve the economy so everyone has a job. Our 'offense' budget is more than the next four countries combined. Unless for our own benefits, do not send soldiers overseas. Today's weapons are missiles and cyber security, so how many soldiers we need?

* If we learn the prediction from the Bible or the endless religious wars, we would not be involved in the Middle East conflict.

Just write down this list at the first sip of coffee. It could be an endless list.

---

5 Our 4T budget for 2020

Our budget for 2020 is 4.7T (1T = 1,000 B). Do we have tax income to cover 4T? As of March 6, 2020 and according to the government budget web site, we do not.

Budget projections for FY 2020	As of 3/6/2020
Outlays	$4.7 Trillion
Revenues	$3.6 Trillion
Deficit	$1.1 Trillion
Debt held by the public (end of FY)	$17.8 Trillion

I bet the numbers have not been updated. As of today (4/4/2020), it would be even worse considering the extra $2 T to fight the Coronavirus, the fast-rising unemployment and the reduced tax revenues from businesses and the capital gains in the stock market.

We need to balance the budget to start with. It is irresponsible to borrow money and ask our children and their children to pay for our debts.

With the huge national debts, the status of the reserve currency of our USD is shaken. We know what happened to the United Kingdom when the pound was replaced by our USD as a reserve currency.

Obama saved the stock market, but doubled our deficit in his terms. He satisfied his voters by giving them what they need. Are we the voters to be blamed? The deficit is important in the long run as we would lose our competitive edge when we have to service the hefty debts. We need to invest in infrastructures, but not in wars.

I propose the following:

1. Add the following in the Constitution. If the president cannot balance the budget, s/he cannot run for the second term.

2. In mid-year, make adjustments to the spending according to the budget / tax income.

Steps to balance the budget:

1. Reduce our burden as a world policeman.

2. Cut down on welfare to ABLE recipients.
3. Cut down on corporate welfare.
4. Prosecute violators such as price gauging by drug companies and disability frauds.

If the U.S. were a corporation, we have bankrupted already.

Filler: How to win the PowerBall

1. Go to the local lottery office and ask to buy all combinations with a check dated today when it is over 500 M. It worked yesterday. If you have more than one PowerBall winner (or someone using the same trick described here), you may have to skip town.

2. Borrow my time machine which is being repaired or the car from "Back to the Future".

Epilogue

This book was written for retirees, beginners and couch potatoes. However, the very basic investing knowledge is expected to avoid another 100 pages. This book has explained how to use the advanced strategies from my other books, but in very simple terms. The 'Do' chapters are the ones you should try them out. To start, use paper testing that should be available from most brokers. Many bonus chapters are your future reading.

Thanks for reading this book and hope it is beneficial to your financial health. If you find this book useful, please write comments 2in the web site you bought the book.

Filler

Relatively speaking (as Einstein said), the US is in far better shape than Japan. Investors should stay away from Japan except the delicious sushi. EU and China and the commodity-rich countries (Russia, Brazil, Australia...) will be in between.

We are not economically better than our parents. Our children will be even worse with loans to pay from our governments.

Appendix 1 – All my books

- Complete the Art of Investing (highly recommended combining most of my books on investing). The Kindle version has over 850 pages (6*9), about 3 times the size of an investing book.
- Sector Rotation: 21 Strategies and another book Shorting (highly recommended for short-term investors) have more specific chapters on the topic and share many articles with "Complete the art of investing".
- Best stocks for 2022 (avail after Dec. 15, 2021).
- "Nuclear War with China".
- Books for today's market: Profit from Coming Market Crash.
- The following books are in a series: Finding Profitable Stocks, Market Timing and Scoring Stocks. Alternate books: Using Fidelity and Using Finviz.
- Books on strategies: "Profit from bull, bear and sideways markets" (Rotation + Momentum + ETF Rotation + trend following), Trading System (similar to printed version of Complete), Swing (Rotation + Momentum), ETF Rotation for Couch Potatoes, Momentum, SuperStocks, Dividend, Penny & Micro Stock, and Retiree.
- Books for advance beginners: Be an expert (highly recommended), Introduce, Investing for Beginners, Beat Fund Managers, Profit via ETFs, Buffett, Ideas, Conservative and Top-Down.
- Miscellaneous: Lessons in Investing. Investing Strategies. Buy Low and Sell High. Buy High and sell Higher. Buffettology. Technical Analysis. Trading Stocks.

Most books have paperbacks. Links and offers are subject to change without notice.

Best stocks to buy for 2022 (avail. after Dec. 15, 21)

We care about performance only. Not considering dividends and fees, my last three books in this series have beaten the SPY (the market to most) by **110%, 71% and 25%** from the publish date to 07/01/2021.

Book	Stocks	Return	Ann.	Beat SPY by
Best Book for 2021 2nd Edition	10	20%	52%	110%
Best Book for 2021	4	29%	52%	71%
Best Book to Buy from Aug, 2020	14	42%	45%	25%
Avg.	9	31%	50%	69%

Appendix 2 - Complete the Art of Investing

Instead of buying 16 books, why not buy one book (Complete the Art of Investing) consisting of 16 books? Besides saving money and your digital shelve space, it gives you quick reference and concentration on the topic you're currently interested in. It covers most investing topics in investing excluding speculative investing such as currency trading and day trading.
The Kindle version has about 850 pages (6*9), about the size of three books of average size. With the cost of $10 and at least 850 investing ideas, it is about one cent per idea. Most other books have only a few ideas in the entire book

The 16 books
This book "Complete Art of Investing" is divided into 16 books as follows. Click for the link to the book described in Amazon.com. I squeezed more than 3,000 pages into 850 pages by eliminating duplicated information such as evaluating stocks.

Book No.	Amazon.com
1	Simple techniques
2	Finding Stocks
3	Evaluating Stocks
4	Scoring Stocks
5	Trading Stocks
6	Market Timing
7	Strategies
8	Sector Rotation
9	Insider Trading
10	Penny Stocks & Micro Cap
11	Momentum Investing
12	Dividend Investing
13	Technical Analysis
14	Investing Ideas
15	The Economy
16	Buffettology

The book links are subject to change without notice.

"How to be a billionaire" is for beginners and couch potatoes, who can use the advanced features of this book in the simplest and less time-consuming techniques. Most advance users can skip this section unless they want to use some of the short cuts described.

We start with the basic books Finding Stocks, Evaluate Stocks, Trading Stocks and Market Timing. You can select and start with one of the many styles and strategies in investing such as swing trading and top-down strategy. Many tools are described in other books such as ETFs, technical analysis, covered calls and trading plan.

Many books start with "Why" to lure you to read more and are followed by "How" and then the theory behind the book.
If the book you're reading is beneficial to you, imagine how it would with 850 pages.

Most readers' comments are on "Debunk the Myths in Investing", which this book is originally based on. As of 2018, I did not know any of the commentators on my books.

"I skipped ahead to his chapter book 14 (of "Complete the Art of Investing"), Investment Advice just to get a feel of his writing style. His research is phenomenal and doesn't overwhelm with big words or catchy "sales-like" tactics.

I truly believe this ordinary man, Mr. Tony Pow, has a gift of explaining his experience as an investor without the bull crap of trying to make you buy his stuff. He seemingly just wants to share his knowledge, tips, and clarity of definitions for the kind of folks like me who want to understand something FIRST before jumping in with emotions of trying to make a boat load of money. I like the technical analysis side he brings.

Mr. Tony Pow talks about hidden gems in his book; well....quite frankly, he is a hidden gem. Thank you and I will also post my comments about this author to my Facebook page!" – JB on this book.

"Excellent book, recommend to all investors... great knowledge. It has fine-tuned my investing strategies... Your book is hard to set aside, as I read it all the time learning good techniques and analysis of stocks, ETF... Since I purchased your book in March, I have underlined, highlighted and placed tabs on top of pages for quick reference." – Aileron on this book.

"Tony, I just finished reading your 2nd edition. It's my pleasure to report that I found it most interesting. You're welcome to use this blurb if you like:

Debunk the Myths in Investing is an all-encompassing look at not only the most salient factors influencing markets and investors, but also a from-the-trenches look at many of the misconceptions and mistakes too many investors make. Reading this book may save not only time and aggravation but money as well!"

Joseph Shaefer, CEO, Stanford Wealth Management LLC.

"Tony, Great work!" from James and Chris, who are portfolio managers.

"'Debunk the Myths in Investing' is a comprehensive book on investing that deals with many aspects of this tense profession in which with a lot of knowledge and a bit of luck (or vice versa) one can greatly benefit...

Therefore 'Debunk the Myths in Investing' is an interesting book that on its 500 pages offer a lot of knowledge related to investing world and many practical advice, so I can recommend its reading if you're interested in this topic."
- Denis Vukosav, Top 500 Reviewers at Amazon.com.

"490 pages (Debunk) of a genius's ranting and hypothesis with various theories throughout, written light-heartedly with ample doses of humor...Yes, the myth of not being able to profitably time the market is BUSTED...

One might ask... Why is he giving away the results of his hard-earned research for only $20? He states that his children are not interested in investing and wants to share his efforts with the world." - Abe Agoda.

"Excellent book, recommend to all investors... great knowledge. It has fine-tuned my investing strategies... Your book is hard to set aside, as I read it all the time learning good techniques and analysis of stocks, ETF... Since I purchased your book in March, I have underlined, highlighted and placed tabs on top of pages for quick reference." - Aileron on this book.

"Great stuff, Tony. It's great to meet experienced traders such as yourself. I had a browse through the book and think your method is a little more refined than mine."

"Your strategy is very rules based and solid. I sometimes envy people who have developed something like this."

Making 50% in one month

I claim to have the best one-month performance ever for recommending 8 or more stocks without using options and leverage. My following return is 57% in a month or 621% annualized. They are slightly different as I calculated the average from the averages of three different accounts. The average buy date is 12/26/18 and the "current date" is 01/28/19.

The performance may not be repeated. I will use the same screen for the coming years and even the expected 10% (or 120% annualized) is very good.

I used the same screen for searching stock candidates. I spent a total of about 20 hours from Dec. 15, 2018 to Jan. 5, 2019.

Stock	Buy Price	Sold or Current Price	Buy date	Sold or Current date	Profit %	Profit % Ann.	Status
CHK	2.13	2.99	01/03/09	01/18/19	40%	982%	Sold
MNK	16.41	21.45	01/03/19	01/25/19	31%	510%	Sold
MNK	16.43	21.45	01/03/19	01/25/19	31%	507%	Sold
NNBR	5.68	8.58	12/26/18	01/28/19	51%	565%	
NNBR	5.72	8.58	12/26/18	01/28/19	66%	727%	
ESTE	4.35	6.45	12/26/18	01/18/19	48%	766%	Sold
LCI	4.61	8.29	12/21/18	01/28/19	80%	767%	
MDR	8.01	9.13	01/08/19	01/28/19	14%	255%	
YRCW	3.29	5.78	12/21/18	01/28/19	76%	727%	
YRCW	3.26	5.78	12/21/18	01/28/19	77%	742%	
ASRT	3.56	4.18	12/26/18	01/28/19	17%	193%	
UTCC	7.13	11.00	12/26/18	01/28/19	54%	600%	
YRCW	2.92	5.78	12/26/18	01/28/19	98%	1083%	

Best one-year return

I claim to have the best-performed article in Seeking Alpha history, an investing site, for recommending 15 or more stocks in one year after the publish date without using options and leverage.

https://seekingalpha.com/article/1095671-amazing-returns-velti-alcatel-lucent-alpha-natural-resources

Your choice

"Complete the art of investing" should be your first choice. If you are short-term trading, I recommend "Sector Rotation: 21 Strategies" and "Shorting Stocks /ETFs". These 3 books together with "Using Fidelity" share many articles.

My recommended stocks can be found in my "Best stocks" series. It would be published on Dec. 15 – it is not a promise. So far, this book and "Sector Rotation: 21 Strategies" are my best sellers. All info are subject to change without notice.

Sector Rotation: 21 Strategies

In addition, as of 5/2020 I bet that no author besides me made **over 4 times** using sector rotation starting the amount more than his yearly salary then.

- On 5/26/2020, I searched for "Sector Rotation" under Amazon's Book. They are listed in the same order except my book Sector Rotation: 21 Strategies.

Book	Date	Size[1]	Kindle $[1]	Hard $
Sector Rotation: 21 Strategies	**05/2020**	**425**	**$9.95**	$24.95
Super Sectors	09/2010	289	$26.39	$49.95
Dual Momentum Investing	11/2014	240	$40.40	$42.20
Sector Investing	05/1996	260		$29.94
Sector Trading Strategies	08/2007	164	$26.39	$16.66
The Sector Strategist	03/2012	225	$26.39	$44.96
ETF Rotation	10/2012	125	**$9.95**	**$14.99**
Optimal... Sector Rotation	07/2015	80		$44.07

[1] From Amazon on size and prices as of 5/25/2020. Last update is 09/2021.

My book won in all categories except the price for hard copy in one. However, my book won as the lowest cost per page by a wide margin.

- I have **21** strategies in sector rotation while most books have only one. It ranges from simple rotation of a stock ETF and cash for beginners to many advanced strategies for experts. Most other books have one or two strategies.
- Andrew, a contributor on Sector Rotation article at Seeking Alpha, said, "Great stuff, Tony. It's great to meet experienced traders such as yourself. I had a browse through the book and think your method is a little more refined than mine."
- "You have written the book in a way that makes good and logical sense." Bill.

- Do not be fooled by past performances. Just check the recent performance of the top 50 stocks selected by IBD in the last five years. The mediocre result (hopefully it will change) could be due to too many followers and/or there is no evergreen strategy.

Sell Short Stocks /ETF

The following is what I did on 09/29/2021. 'Return' is similar to above.

Stocks	Short Date	Close date	Duration	Return	Annualized
ACVA	06/10/21	09/29/21	111	22%	72%
CCL	07/14/21	09/29/21	77	-8%	-36%
CENX	09/17/21	09/29/21	12	3%	105%
CLOV	09/16/21	09/29/21	13	10%	291%
CSPR	09/16/21	09/29/21	13	33%	917%
EOSE	09/15/21	09/29/21	14	10%	261%
MILE	07/22/21	09/29/21	69	53%	279%
NCLH	07/27/21	09/29/21	64	-5%	-27%
REAL	06/04/21	09/29/21	117	22%	68%
UAVS	06/04/21	09/29/21	117	41%	127%
Average	07/30/21	09/29/21	61	18%	206%
RSP				0%	-1%

Appendix 3 - Our window to the investing world

The paperback version of this chapter can be found in the following link.
http://ebmyth.blogspot.com/2013/11/web-sites.html

- **General**
  Wikipedia / Investopedia /Yahoo!Finance / MarketWatch / Cnnfn / Morningstar /CNBC / Bloomberg / WSJ / Barron's / Motley Fool / TheStreet

- **Evaluate stocks**
  Finviz / SeekingAlpha / MSN Money / Zacks / Daily Finance / ADR / Fidelity / Earnings Impact / OpenInsider / NYSE /

NASDAQ / SEC / SEC for 10K and 10Q (quarterly) reports required to file for listed stocks in major exchanges.

- **Charts**
  BigCharts / FreeStockCharts / StockCharts /

- **Screens**
  Yahoo!Finance / Finviz / CNBC / Morningstar /

- **Besides stocks**
  123Jump / Hoover's Online / FINRA Bond Market Data / REIT / Commodity Futures / Option Industry

- **Vendors**
  AAII / Zacks / IBD / GuruFocus / VectorVest / Fidelity / Interactive Brokers / Merrill Lynch /

- **Economy.**
  Econday / EcoconStats / Federal Reserve / Economist /

- **Misc.**
  Dow Jones Indices / Russell / Wilshire / IRS / Wikinvest / ETF Database / ETF Trends / Nolo (estate planning) / AARP /

Appendix 4 - ETFs / Mutual Funds

What is an ETF

ETFs have basic differences from mutual funds: 1. Lower management expenses, 2. Trade ETFs same as stocks, and 3. Usually more diversified but not more selective than the related mutual funds such as NOBL vs FRDPX.

The major classifications of ETFs are 1. Simulating an index such as SPY, QQQ and DIA, 2. Simulating a sector such as XLE and SOXX, 3. Simulating an asset class such as GLD and SLV, 4. Simulating a country or a group of countries such as EWC and FXI, 5. Managed by a manager(s) such as ARKK, 6. Betting a market or sector to go down such as SH and PSQ, and 7. Leveraged (not recommended for beginners).

Fidelity: Index ETFs (https://www.fidelity.com/etfs/overview).
Wikipedia on ETF (http://en.wikipedia.org/wiki/Exchange-traded_fund).

List of ETFs

ETF database (Recommended): http://etfdb.com/
ETF Bloomberg: http://www.bloomberg.com/markets/etfs/
ETF Trends: http://www.etftrends.com/
A list of ETFs. Seeking Alpha.
http://etf.stock-encyclopedia.com/category/)
A list of contra ETFs (or bear ETFs)
http://www.tradermike.net/inverse-short-etfs-bearish-etf-funds/
Misc.: ETFGuide, ETFReplay
Fidelity low-cost index funds:
https://www.youtube.com/watch?v=zpKi4_IJvlY
Fidelity Annuity funds with performance data.
http://fundresearch.fidelity.com/annuities/category-performance-annual-total-returns-quarterly/FPRAI?refann=005

Other resources

Most subscription services offer research on ETFs. IBD has a strategy dedicated to ETFs and so does AAII to name a couple.

Seeking Alpha has extensive resources for ETF including an ETF screener and investing ideas. So is ETFdb.

Not all ETFs are created equal
Check their performances and their expenses.

When to use or not to use ETFs
I prefer sector mutual funds in some industries, as they have many bad stocks such as drug industry, banks, miners and insurers. Most mutual funds cannot time the market.

When you believe a sector is heading up (or contra ETF for heading down), but you do not have time to do research on specific stocks, buy an ETF for the sector; it is same for the market.

Half ETF
Taking out half of the stocks that score below the average in an index ETF could beat the same full ETF itself. I call it HETF (half the ETF). You heard it here first. To illustrate, sort the expected P/E (not including stocks with negative earnings) in ascending order and only include the stocks on the first half. Add more fundamental metrics. It will take a few minutes.

Disadvantages of ETFs
- When you have two stocks in a sector ETF one good one and one bad one, the ETF treats them the same. Stock pickers would buy the one that has a better appreciation potential.
- Sometimes the return could be misleading due to stock rotation. To illustrate this, on August 29, 2012, SHLD was replaced by LYB in a sector fund. SHLD was down by 4% and LYB was up by 4% primarily due to the switch. Unless you sell and buy at the right time (which is impossible), your return would not match the ETF's returns due to the replacement.
- Ensure the performance matches the corresponding index; it is hard due to excluding dividends.

Advantages of ETFs
- We have demonstrated that you can beat the market by using market timing. Between 2000 and Nov., 2013, you only exit and reenter the market 3 times and the result is astonishing.
- It is easy to rotate a sector vs. buying/selling all of the stocks in this sector. Rotating a sector is the same as trading a stock.
- The risk is spread out, and your portfolio is diversified especially for a market ETF or buying three or more ETFs in different sectors.

- Periodically the bad stocks in most funds are replaced by better stocks.
- Eliminate the time in researching stocks.

Leveraged ETFs

I do not recommend them. Some are 2x, 3x and even higher. They're too risky for beginners. However, when you are very sure or your tested strategy has very low drawdown, you may want to use them to improve performance. Most leveraged ETFs and contra ETFs have higher fees.

My basic ETF tables

I include some contra ETFs, mutual funds and Fidelity's annuity. Some of these may be interesting to you.

ETFs and funds come and go. Some ideas and classifications are my own interpretation. Refer to ETFdb for updated information. Not responsible for any error. Check out the ETF or fund before you take any action.

Table by market cap:

Category	ETF	Mutual Funds	Fidelity's Annuity	Contra ETF	Alternate
Size:					
Large Cap	DIA	See Blend		DOG	
	SPY			SH	FXAIX VOO
	QQQ			PSQ	FNCMX
	RYH				
Blend	IWD	BEQGX			
Growth	SPYG	FBGRX			FSPGX
Value	SPYV	DOGGX			FLCOX
Dividend	NOBL	FRDPX			
	VYM				
Mid Cap			FNBSC	MYY	
Blend	MDY	VSEQX			
Growth		STDIX			
		BPTRX			
Value		FSMVX			
Small Cap			FPRGC	SBB	FSSNX
Blend	IWM	HDPSX			
Growth		PRDSX			FECGX

Value		SKSEX			FISVX
Micro	IWC				
Multi					
Blend		VDEOX			
Growth		VHCOX			
Value		TCLCX			
Total					FSKAX
Bond					
Long Term (20)	VLV	BTTTX		TBF	
Mid Term (7 – 10)	VCIT	FSTGX			
Short Term (1 – 3 yrs.)	VCSH	THOPX			
Total	BOND	PONDX			
Corp Invest Grade	VCIT	NTHEX			
High Yield (junk)	PHB	SPHIX			
Muni	MUB	Check state			
Special situation					
Buy back	PKW				

Table by sectors:

Sector	**ETF**	**Mutual Funds**	**Fidelity's Annuity**
Banking[1]		FSRBK	
Regional	IAT		
Bio Tech	IBB	FBIOX	
	XBI	Large	
Consumer Dis.	XLY	FSCPX	FVHAC
Consumer Staple	XLP	FDFAX	FCSAC
Finance	KIE	FIDSX	FONNC
	IYF		
Energy	XLE	FSENX	FJLLC
Energy Service		FSESX	
Gold	GLD	FSAGX	
Gold Miner	GDX	VGPMX	

Health Care	IYH	FSPHX	FPDRC
	VHT	VGHCX	
House Builder	ITB	FSHOX	
	ITB	Perform	
Industrial	IYJ	FCYIX	FBALC
Material	VAW	FSDPX	
	IYM		
Oil	USO		
Oil Service	OIH	FSESX	
Oil Exploration	XOP		
Real Estate	VNQ	FRIFX	FFWLC
REIT	VNQ		
Retail	RTH	FSRPX	
	XRT		
Regional bank	KRE	FSRBX	
Semi Conduct	SMH		
Software	XSW	FSCSX	
	IGV		
Technology	XLK	FSPTX	FYENC
	FDN	FBSOX	
		ROGSX	
Telecomm.	VOX	FSTCX	FVTAC
Transport	XTN		
	IYT		
Utilities	XLU	FSUTX	FKMSC
Wireless		FWRLX	

Footnote. [1] Also check Finance.

Table by countries outside the USA:

Country	ETF	Mutual Funds	Fidelity's Annuity	Alternate
Australia	EWA			
Brazil	EWZ			
Canada	EWC	FICDX		
China	FXI	FHKCX		
EAFE	EFA			
Emerging	VWO	FEMEX	FEMAC	FPADX
Europe	VGK	FIEUX		
Global	KXI	PGVFX		
Greece	GREK			
India	INDY	MINDX		
Indonesia	EIDO			
Latin America	ILF	FLATX		
Nordic		FNORX		
Hong Kong	EWH			
Japan	EWJ	FJPNX		
S. Africa	EZA			
S. Korea	EWY	MAKOX		
Singapore	EWS			
Taiwan	EWT			
	TUR			
United Kingdom	EWU			
Foreign:				
Combination				
Intern. Div.	IDV			FTIHX
Small Cap	SCZ			
Value	EFV			
Europe	VGK			

#Filler: Honey, my book can play music.

https://www.youtube.com/watch?v=HxGT5z6d-GA&list=PLMZa6mP7jZ2b1otqG4tfbgZpLEdh6YiNF

It may cut down commercials by casting it to TV.

www.ingramcontent.com/pod-product-compliance
Lightning Source LLC
Chambersburg PA
CBHW030621220526
45463CB00004B/1370

* 9 7 8 1 6 9 9 2 6 1 4 6 0 *